Mrs Scry Yorkshire Pye

Valerie Wood (signature)

A Collection of Yorkshire Recipes

Compiled by Valerie Wood

Illustrations by
Peter and Catherine Wood

Hutton Press
1996

Published by

The Hutton Press Ltd.,
130 Canada Drive, Cherry Burton,
Beverley, East Yorkshire HU17 7SB.

Printed by
Image Colourprint Ltd.,
Willerby, Hull.

ISBN 1872167 83 7

CONTENTS

ACKNOWLEDGEMENTS

Mrs Gertrude Attwood, Hull, for loan of family recipe books.
Mrs Muriel Codd, Leven, for loan of family recipe books.
David Harris, North Newbald, for loan of old postcards and newspapers.
Chris Ketchell, Local History Unit, Hull College, Park St,
Hull, for permission to use Mrs Marshall's recipes and
syllabus of Women's Industries.
Local History Unit and Science Department, Central Library,
Hull, for permission to use old recipe books.
County Archives Office, East Riding Council, Beverley.
Permission to use old manuscripts and Robert Spofforth's Book.
Mrs Joyce Mills, Tadcaster and Mrs Irene Howling, Leeds,
for loan of old recipes.
Mr R. P. Prior, Heaton Mersey, for loan of his grandmother's recipe book.
Mr Sherry, Hull. for the gift of his recipe book.
Mr Norman Stockton, Driffield, East Riding Dialect Society,
for his book of Economical Recipes, 1916.
Mrs Mavis Taylor, for old remedies.
Mr D Thomas, Halifax, for loan of his mother's recipe books
and home hints, in particular the Book of Recipes from
Sowerby Bridge, 1907.
Many thanks are also due to those who were kind enough to
loan material, but which, because of lack of space or
duplication of recipes has not been used.

Introduction

The idea of compiling a book of Yorkshire recipes occurred to me as I was writing my first novel, THE HUNGRY TIDE, when I created the eighteenth century character of Mrs Scryven.

I imagined her as a bustling little body, completely enveloped in a huge white apron with a white cap upon her head. She was a countrywoman who used the vegetables, meat, fish or fowl which were available locally, and above all she used the herbs which grew in her garden and the Holderness countryside, for cooking and for remedies.

As her character grew so did the urge to create and research into the old Receipts, and together Mrs Scryven and I came up with several recipes and remedies including Mrs Scryven's Yorkshire Pye, which consisted of a topping of thick golden crust hiding deep layers of tender pigeon flavoured with sweet bay and lovage, a guaranteed cure, she insisted, for a weary traveller.

She made steaming gruel and bramble tarts, cooked game pie, baked her own bread, kept her own pig and milked her own 'coo'!

The art of cookery has occupied the thoughts of man and woman since fire was discovered and the cooking pot invented, and although I don't intend this book to be a history of cooking as I am neither a professional cook nor historian, I do, like the majority of people, love good food, and I find the concept of changes in cooking and eating habits quite fascinating.

According to fifteenth century cookery books the richer members of the English community of that time were eating whale, peacock, curlew, crane and heron, swan as well as duck, plover and venison. Nothing, it seemed was sacred, not even the sweet singing lark; anything which flew or swam, was destined for the pot or fire. Agricultural workers on the other hand lived chiefly on barley cakes, onions and beer.

Eating habits were changing in the eighteenth and nineteenth centuries and the French chefs with their exotic breads and sweet cakes and artistic presentation were amused at the English for their taste in such mundane offerings as sheep's head and pig's trotters, beef and mutton pies, rook pie, kidney pudding and pea soup.

For desserts, sweet tarts of rhubarb, apples, cherries and damsons were becoming popular as was plum duff. New vegetables appeared, marrow and pumpkin, and the tomato or 'love apple,' arrived from North Carolina.

In the nineteenth century Bryan Donkin of the Dartford Iron Works was making tinned containers for preserving food, but it is doubtful if the contemporaries of Mrs Scryven would use such a newfangled invention but would be content with bottling fruit for the winter months, and making jams and jellies, pickles and chutneys with any surplus.

The nineteenth century also brought in the typical 'English Breakfast,' when those who could afford it ate indulgently of porridge, smoked fish, bacon and eggs, toast and marmalade, and topped it off with a jug of coffee or pot of tea. Those who couldn't afford such luxuries ate bread, onions and drank ale, so it seems that in four centuries, for some people, nothing much had changed!

So my mission here is to give you a concept of Yorkshire cooking which I have gleaned from family and friends, and from recipes which have been kindly sent to me; from old Receipt Books which have been lent to me or which I have studied in libraries and council archives. These I hope will stir some long lost remembrance or indeed induce you to put on the oven and create future memories for others. So why not start this book with the Staff of Life, without which, rich or poor, we would be at a loss to replace.

Valerie Wood
June 1996

Tea had become the most popular form of beverage and in the North gave its name in genteel circles to 'Afternoon Tea,' in which cake and scones and bread and butter and jam were served and which in time became established for the working classes also, with dinner at midday as the main meal of the day.

•

My love of food I trace back to childhood, for haven't we all fond memories of food given in love and comfort and taken with pleasure? Of bread fresh from the oven and drizzling with golden syrup, of 'soldiers' dipped in soft boiled egg, of steaming hot soup to warm a snowball warrier, apple pie with thick golden custard, tender beef stew with dumplings; fish cakes, meat pies and mushy peas, vinegary cockles eaten on the sea front at Scarborough, rosy apples spun with crisp toffee on Guy Fawkes Night. These are my memories; you, I'm sure will have yours.

Breads

When I was a child my granny used to send me for a 'ha'porth' of yeast before I went to school in a morning. As I walked back from the grocer's shop I would dip my fingers into the moist creamy texture and nibble the flavour which was like no other, and Granny would look into the paper bag and grumble at the short measure!

She would froth the yeast, knead the dough, pounding it on the kitchen table, and set it to rise in the deep stoneware pancheon in front of the kitchen range, and on returning home at teatime I would be greeted by the wonderful aroma of freshly baked bread which we ate spread with golden syrup or jam.

Today it is possible to make bread with the help of electric mixers and quick rise dried yeast granules. This I do regularly and it makes very good bread, but sometimes, for old times sake, I knead by hand and let memory and time roll back. As a special welcome for family and friends as they step through the door, there is nothing to beat the smell and sight of newly baked bread.

KNEADING THE DOUGH BY HAND. Place the dough on a flat surface then stretch away from you, using the heel of your hand or knuckles. Then lift the edges back to the middle and repeat. Keep turning the dough and repeat the process until the dough begins to feel springy. Kneading by hand is both therapeutic and relaxing, and if you are feeling tense or frustrated pummelling the dough is a good way of getting rid of anger!

'KNOCKING BACK' — This means pounding the dough to remove all the gas out of the dough and bring it back to its original size. It is then allowed to rise for a second time.

Always cover the dough completely, either with a clean damp tea towel or a greased polythene bag. If you don't, a skin will develop and spoil the texture.

Bread dough will rise even if left in a cool place. If you want to make it the night before it is required, leave it to rise, covered, overnight in a larder or the bottom of the 'fridge, then knead and shape the next morning in the usual way. The bread will be as good if not better for a longer rising time.

BAKING — Ovens vary, so it is difficult to lay down rules, but essentially, an oven needs to be hot (425F 220C approx or Gas Mark 7) to start with and can then be lowered.

Plain White Bread

This is a recipe in regular use at our house. It is delicious, nutritious and easy. A hot oven is required and temperatures may vary, so get to know your oven. Best results come from good strong 'bread' flour. The ingredients listed here make 2 1lb loaves or cobs or 15/18 breadcakes.

1 1/2 lb strong white flour
1/2 teaspoon salt
1sachet easy blend dried yeast or 1/2 oz fresh yeast
3/4 pt hand hot water
2 tablespoons sunflour oil or small knob of lard

Warm the mixing bowl.

Pour the hot water into a jug and add the sunflower oil or lard.

Put the flour into the warmed bowl, stir in the salt and the yeast granules and pour in the oiled water. (If using fresh yeast, before adding to the flour, first dissolve the yeast in a cupful of the measured water with a pinch of sugar and allow to froth). Knead the ingredients together for 10/15 minutes adding a little more water or flour if required, until the dough is smooth and elastic. If using a mixer and dough hook the time taken will be halved. Cover the dough and the bowl completely with a clean damp tea towel and leave to rise in a warm place for approximately 1 hour or until the dough has doubled in size.

In the meantime grease and flour the loaf tins or trays.

Knock back or punch the dough to remove the yeast gases and knead again for 5/10 minutes. The dough should feel smooth and pliable and nice to handle. Turn on to a floured board and divide and shape into loaves, cobs or breadcakes. Half fill the loaf tins, or place the cobs or breadcakes onto the trays, cover again and leave to prove once more until well risen (approximately 3/4 hour). Place in the centre of a hot oven 450F. 225C. Gas No. 7 then lower slightly after 5 minutes. Loaves take approximately 40 minutes, breadcakes about 15/20 minutes. Rap the bottom of the loaf to test if ready, it should sound hollow. The breadcakes should be well risen and golden.

Cool on a wire rack.

Eat with pleasure !

Quick Wholemeal Bread

This recipe I use when I am short of time, which is often! It is quick and easy and wholesome. I use half wholemeal flour and half strong white as this makes a lighter texture. It is kneaded only once and the ingredients used here make 2 small loaves or cobs or 15/18 rolls.

3/4 lb wholemeal flour
3/4 lb strong white flour
2 tsp salt
1 sachet easy blend dried yeast or 1 oz fresh yeast
3/4 pint hand hot water
2 tablespoons sunflower oil or small knob of lard
2 level teaspoons sugar

Warm the mixing bowl and grease and flour the tins or trays. Pour the hot water into a jug and add the sunflower oil or lard.

Put the two flours into the warmed bowl and stir until well blended. Stir in the salt, sugar and yeast granules and pour in the oiled water and mix to a soft dough.(If using fresh yeast, before adding to the flour, first dissolve the yeast in 1/2 cupful of the measured water with 1/2 tsp of the sugar)

Turn onto a floured board and knead by hand for about 10 minutes. By mixer and dough hook this takes about 4 minutes. Shape into loaves, half filling the prepared tins, or make into cobs or breadcakes. Cover completely with a clean damp tea towel and leave to prove in a warm place until well risen, approximately 3/4 hour.

Place in the centre of a hot oven 475 F 240C Gas Mark 8/9 for 5 minutes then reduce the temperature to 400F 200C Gas Mark 6. Bake loaves or cobs for about 35 minutes until risen and golden. Rolls or breadcakes take about 15 minutes. The base of the loaves should sound hollow when cooked. If, like me you like a crusty loaf, return them to the oven out of the tins and crisp on the oven shelf for 5 minutes.

Cool on a wire rack.

Then eat with butter or your favourite spread, with cheese or jam or honey and know that bread really is the staff of life.

Special Breads

Once you have become proficient at making plain bread, why not experiment? Use sunflower or pumpkin seed, make a milk or oaten loaf, or add sugar and currants for a Yorkshire Teacake or try your hand at plaiting the dough, like the ones seen at Harvest Festivals. There's nothing quite so pleasing as a table full of cottage loaves, Yorkshire Teacakes, crusty cobs or breakfast rolls, all golden and fragrant and fresh from the oven. But be warned, they won't stay on the table for long!

Sunflower Seed Bread Buns

1 oz sunflower seed
  or a
1/2 oz pumpkin seed

Use either the plain white or wholemeal recipe as given but before adding the oiled water, stir in the seed and mix well. Make in the usual way and shape into buns. Take enough dough to fit in the palm of your hand and roll into a ball. Put onto the greased tray and flatten slightly with the heel of your hand.

Bake in the centre of a hot oven for 15/20 minutes. Cool on a wire tray.

These are especially nice eaten with cheese and pickle.

Yorkshire Teacakes

1lb strong white flour
1/2 teaspoon salt
2 oz sugar
1 tablespoon sunflower oil or small knob butter
1 sachet easy blend dried yeast or 1/2 oz fresh yeast
4 oz currants
1/2 pint warm milk
pinch nutmeg (optional)

Warm the mixing bowl

Pour the warm milk into a jug and add the sunflower oil or butter. Put the flour into the warmed bowl, stir in the salt, sugar and nutmeg, sprinkle in the dried yeast and pour in the oiled milk. (If using fresh yeast, before adding to the flour, first ferment the yeast in 1/2 cup of hand hot water with a pinch of sugar).

Knead the ingredients together for 10/15 minutes until the dough is smooth. If using a mixer and dough hook the time taken will be halved. Cover the dough and the bowl completely with a clean damp tea towel and leave to rise in a warm place for 1 hour.

Grease and flour the baking trays and prepare the oven to reach 400/450 F. 200/230 C. Gas Mark 6/7.

Knock back, add the dried fruit and mix in well. Knead again for 10 minutes, keeping the dough soft and warm and pliable. Turn onto a floured board and divide the dough into 10 equal pieces, shape into round flat cakes and place on the trays with space between so that they don't touch.

Cover and put to prove and rise in a warm place, and when plump and risen to about an inch, bake in the centre of the oven for 20 minutes.

Cool on a wire tray, then split with your fingers and savour the aroma.

Yule Cakes

3 lb flour
3/4 lb lard
1 lb currants
1 lb sultanas
1 lb sugar
1 egg
1 teaspoon baking powder
1 1/2 oz yeast
a little candied peel
flavour with mixed spice and mix with a little milk.

Rub the lard into the flour. Rise yeast as for teacakes. Add other ingredients. Make into rounds like teacakes and bake about half an hour in a moderate oven. Delicious when eaten with cheese.

This is an old recipe, halve ingredients if necessary.

Harvest Plait

Make the plain white or wholemeal dough and after the final kneading, roll out the dough into an oblong to fit your baking board.

Divide into three equal strips, leaving the dough joined at the top and plait as you would the hair of a schoolgirl. Tuck the ends under and place on a greased and floured baking tray. Brush with milk or a light egg wash, cover and leave to prove and rise in a warm place.

Lightly wash again and scatter a few poppy seeds over for decoration.

Bake in a hot oven as for plain white or wholemeal bread for 20/30 minutes.

Cool on a wire tray.

Yorkshire Cob

Using the same recipe as before, for white or wholemeal, shape into a large round, place on a greased and floured tray and with a sharp knife cut into the centre of the dough, making a slit about 1" deep. Cover, prove and rise.

Bake in centre of hot oven for 30 minutes approximately.

Cool on a wire tray.

Oaten Bread

In my early days of experimenting with dough, I was very much a 'hit or miss' baker; the recipe given here was accidental in as much that one day I ran out of wholemeal flour and substituted oatmeal instead. It proved to be successful in terms of flavour and it has since been perfected enough to become a firm favourite, especially when eaten for Sunday breakfast with grilled bacon and eggs. However, during my research into Yorkshire recipes I discovered that at least two centuries ago, the oat cereal, being grown here in Yorkshire, was always used in bread making and was included in many forms of baking.

4 oz medium oatmeal
1/2 lb strong white bread flour
1/2 lb wholemeal flour
1 sachet easy blend dried yeast or 1 oz fresh yeast
1/2 pint warm milk
1/4 pint hand hot water
1 teaspoon sugar
2 teaspoons salt
1 teaspoon honey
2 tablespoons sunflower oil or knob of butter

Warm the mixing bowl. Pour the hot water and warm milk into a jug and add the honey and sunflower oil or butter. Put the two flours and oatmeal into the bowl and mix well, stir in the salt and sugar, sprinkle in the yeast and pour in the oiled and honeyed water. (If using fresh yeast, first ferment the yeast in a cupful of the measured liquid). Mix well and knead on a flat surface for about 10 minutes or until the dough is smooth, firm and pliable. You may need a drop more milk as the oatmeal absorbs more liquid; by mixer and dough hook the time should be halved.

Return to the bowl and cover completely. Leave in a warm place to prove and rise for about an hour or possibly more. Grease and flour 2 trays and prepare the oven to reach 450 F 230 C. Gas Mark 8.

Knock back and punch out the air and knead for 5 minutes then divide the dough in half and shape each piece into a rough round cob, sprinkle with oatmeal and place on individual greased trays. With a sharp knife make a deep slash in each cob, about 1/2" deep.

Cover and prove and rise in a warm place for 30/40 minutes. Bake in the hot oven for 20 minutes, then lower the temperature to 375/400 F. 190/200 C. Gas Mark 5/6 for a further 10 minutes. Be sure to tap the base to check if cooked. Leave at lower temperature for a further 10 minutes if in doubt. Cool on a wire tray.

Soups

"Beautiful Soup, so rich and green,
Waiting in a hot tureen.
Who for such dainties would not stoop?
Soup of the evening, beautiful Soup!"

So sang the Mock Turtle in Lewis Carroll's Alice in Wonderland. And small wonder that he sobbed for here is a nineteenth century recipe from **Mrs Marshall's Cookery Book**

Mock Turtle Soup

Half a calf's head
six quarts of stock
one carrot, one turnip, one leek, two onions, celery, plus
eight cloves
four blades of mace
twelve peppercorns
four wineglasses of sherry

And simmer for four hours. After straining, removing fat, clarifying and skinning, you then cut out the meat and stamp out with a small round cutter, wash and add to the soup. The remains of the head can be used for entrees.

And perhaps your sympathies lie with the poor turtle for he was once a real turtle, and here is a recipe for

Clear Turtle Soup

Take one pound of sun dried turtle and soak it in cold water for three days, constantly changing the water, then put it to cook for ten to twelve hours in good stock and with all kinds of vegetables, such as for each quart, a little celery, one small carrot, one turnip, one leek, two bayleaves, two onions and herbs, including basil and marjoram, thyme, parsley, three cloves, a blade of mace, six black and white peppercorns, a good dust of coralline pepper and two Jamaica peppercorns tied up in a piece of muslin; keep it gently simmering, adding more stock as that in the pot reduces. When the turtle is cooked, strain off the stock, remove any fat, let it cool, then clarify and strain.

Home made soup is evocative of comfort and caring. It brings us memories of winter warming chicken broth, of thick onion soup guaranteed to chase colds away; of creamy leek and potato, green peas or carrot. Soup can be made from practically any fresh vegetable, except perhaps runner bean which has too strong a flavour.

And what of those long hot days of summer when for our lunch we can enjoy chilled tomato or mushroom soup served with the bread we have made ourselves and a tossed green salad.

Chicken Broth

This soup I have made for many years. I have never had a recipe, it just evolved, and it is different every time I make it for I use whatever vegetables there are to hand, sometimes substituting carrot for caulifower, swede for potato, leek for onion, but I always add herbs for that special flavour and sometimes a clove of garlic.

Cooked chicken carcass
1 large onion or small leek
2 carrots
1 parsnip
2 medium size potatoes
Large handful of chopped mixed fresh herbs
marjoram/tarragon/parsley.
1 tablespoon of sunflower oil
1 tablespoon of plain flour
salt & pepper to taste.
1 clove of peeled and chopped garlic

Put the chicken carcass left over from a previous meal into a large saucepan, cover with water to 3/4 full. Put on the lid and bring to the boil, then turn down the heat and simmer for about an hour or until all the meat has fallen off the bone.

Cool, then take out all the bones and pieces of gristle and skim off the fat.

Chop the vegetables into small pieces and fry gently in the sunflower oil for 2/3 minutes to seal in the flavour, add the chopped herbs and the garlic if used and cook for further 2 minutes. Add the flour and stir to absorb the oil and thicken. Remove from heat and stir into the broth.

Simmer for further 10 minutes or until the vegetables are at the desired tenderness. Add seasoning to taste.

Serve in deep bowls and eat with thick slices of wholemeal bread.

Mushrooms and Hazelnut Soup

This is a great favourite of ours and can be eaten hot or chilled. I like to think that I would get up as dawn is breaking and wander into the dew drenched fields and pick the newly opened Field mushrooms. In practical terms it isn't always possible and we have to be sure of our mushrooms or risk having a tummy upset!

But supermarkets and local shops all stock good quality fresh mushrooms, and we can handpick from the shelf without getting our feet wet! Don't ever use wet or 'manky' ones that have been left over for a few days. For this soup you will need either a blender or a sieve.

12 oz chopped fresh mushrooms
1 medium onion chopped
3/4 pint of water
3/4 pint of milk
3 oz hazelnuts
2 ozs butter
1/4 pint single cream
salt & pepper to taste
parsley

Cook the onion in butter until soft. Add nuts and mushrooms, and fry for two minutes. Add the water and milk, bring almost to the boil, lower heat, cover and simmer for 30 minutes. Whiz in an electric blender or press through a sieve until smooth, add cream and seasoning. Return to the pan and reheat carefully. Do not let it boil.

Serve hot or cold, preferably in white or cream bowls for effect and garnish with a sprinkling of parsley.

Leek and Potato Soup

This must be the most economical of all soups to make; it is extremely nourishing and will happily simmer away whilst you are busy with other things.

4 fat sliced and chopped leeks
2 large diced potatoes
1 small chopped onion
1 1/2 pints vegetable or chicken stock
1/2 pint milk
salt and black pepper to taste
2 tablespoons sunflower oil or 2 oz butter
Large handful of fresh herbs
1 small sprig of mint
pinch of paprika

In a large heavy based saucepan melt the butter or oil, add the leeks, potatoes, onion and herbs and stir until well coated. Put the lid on the pan and turn the heat right down so that the vegetables sweat without burning for about 10 minutes.

Add the stock and the milk, bring to simmering point and cook for about 30 minutes until tender. Season generously with salt and freshly ground black pepper and you can now eat it just as it is, thick and wholesome or blend to a puree with either a liquidiser or sieve. Serve with chopped mint for garnish and a sprinkling of paprika.

Pea Soup with bacon and herbs

From an unsigned manuscript. 1811

2 1/2 cups of old peas
10 cups of stock
1/4 1lb piece bacon
1lb chopped sorrel
2 endives - sliced
1/2 cup chopped spearmint
2 ozs butter
1/4 cup cream

Boil the peas in the stock with the bacon, sorrel, endive and spearmint. When the peas are tender, remove the bacon and chop it into small dice. Put the soup through a food mill or sieve and return it to the cleaned pan. Reheat, stir in the butter and cream, add a little pepper and then put back the chopped bacon. Pour into a tureen and serve.

This soup works equally well with frozen garden peas and young spinach leaves and slightly less cream if desired.

Fifteenth century cookery book.   1420 AD
Lange Wortes de pesoun.
Take grene pesyn an wash hem clene an cast hem on a potte, an boyle hem tyle hey breste.

Cream of Lentil Soup

Mrs Ann Ainsley, Thorne

1/4 lb lentils
1 large carrot
1 large onion
1 celery stalk
1/2 small turnip
1 medium potato
1 pint milk
1/2 pint chicken stock or water
handful of parsley
pinch of grated nutmeg
1 tablespoon cooking oil or small knob of margarine
salt and pepper
cream

Wash lentils and drain. Thinly slice carrots, onion and celery, cut turnip and potato into small dice and fry together gently in oil or margarine for 7-10 minutes. Add lentils and parsley. Pour in milk and stock or water. Simmer very gently for 1 hour. Sieve and return to pan, add grated nutmeg and seasoning to taste. Reheat and just before serving add cream and garnish with parsley.

Cream of Potato Soup

Mrs Ann Ainsley, Thorne

1 lb potatoes
1 large onion
2 medium celery stalks
3/4 pint water
1 level teaspoon salt
shake of pepper
1 oz cornflour
1/2 pint milk
2 level tablespoons finely chopped parsley
1 tablespoon olive oil

Dice potatoes, thinly slice onion and celery and fry in olive oil for 10 minutes without browning. Add water, salt and pepper and bring to the boil. Cover pan and simmer for 45 minutes. Liquidise and return to pan. Mix cornflour to smooth paste with a little cold milk, add remainder of milk and add to soup. Simmer for 5 minutes. Ladle into bowls and sprinkle with parsley.

Cream of Cauliflower Soup

Mrs Ann Ainsley, Thorne

Follow recipe for Potato soup but use 1 lb cauliflower divided into small florets instead of potato. Add large pinch nutmeg with salt and pepper.

Fish

Hull and the East Coast has long been known for its fishing trade. Hull was a centre for whaling as long ago as the 16th century and fishing for cod was already established. In 1843 2000 tons of fish were caught off Flamborough and sent to Hull by road and then on to the West Riding of Yorkshire.

Scarborough fishing smacks were also successful and the Scarborough market was besieged by fishermen from Brixham and Ramsgate who moved into the North Sea – then known as the German Ocean – anxious to participate in the prolific haul of plaice, sole and haddock.

The North Sea had, and still has, an infamous reputation among those who sail it; cunning, tricky and devious with powerful tides and changeable currents. The long and exposed coastline can be hidden from view in an instant when vaporous sea frets descend, and it is not a sea to be undertaken lightheartedly; which perhaps we sometimes forget as we tuck into our fish dishes.

Bill's Mackerel

Bill, who lives in the old market town of Hedon, fishes off the East Coast, sometimes going up as far as Whitby to catch herring. His favourite dish though, is mackerel, freshly caught, cleaned and gutted and cooked under the grill until just tender. I have added my own version of gooseberry sauce in which I add the feathery herb of dill or fennel.

Slit the fish with a sharp knife along the belly from behind the gills to just above the tail. Scrape out the entrails and rinse under cold water. The head and tail can be left on when cooking whole or otherwise cut off with a sharp knife. Use scissors to cut off the fins and gills.

Turn grill to high, brush fish with butter and place on grill pan, turn heat down to medium as fish starts to sizzle. Cook for about 8 minutes each side.

Gooseberry sauce a sharp sauce for oily fish

1/2 lb gooseberries
2 oz sugar
1 tablespoon water
2 teaspoons chopped dill or fennel

Simmer the gooseberries, sugar, herbs and water in a pan until the berries split. Remove from the heat and mash with a fork or puree in a blender; when cool put into a dish and serve with the mackerel.

Caty's Fish Pie

1 1/2 lb smoked haddock
1/2 lb white fish - cod/haddock
1 pint milk
4 ozs butter/margarine
1 bay leaf
2 ozs flour
2 chopped hard boiled eggs
4 tablespoons chopped parsley
1 tablespoon capers — optional
1 tablespoon lemon juice
salt & pepper

Topping
2 1/2 lb boiled potatoes
2 ozs butter or cream
4 tablespoons milk
1 oz grated Swaledale cheese

Preheat the oven to 400 F. 200 C. Gas Mark 6

Place the fish in an ovenproof dish and pour over half the milk. Add the bay leaf and a few small knobs of the butter and bake for about 15 minutes. Pour off the liquid and reserve, then skin the fish and flake the flesh. Melt the remaining butter/margarine in a saucepan, stir in the flour and gradually add the fish liquid, stirring constantly. Add the remaining milk, salt and pepper and simmer for 3 or 4 minutes. Next, mix the fish pieces, sauce, hard boiled eggs, parsley and capers if used, stir in the lemon juice and return to a buttered dish.

Cream the potatoes with milk and butter, season with salt and pepper, adding cream for an extra delicious flavour. Spread over the fish mixture, forking a pattern on top, and sprinkle with grated cheese. Bake at same temperature as before for about 20/30 minutes until the top is crisp.

Serve with green peas or runner beans and carrots.

Fish Cake

Mrs Sayers (Economical Recipes 1916)

5 ozs mashed potato
1/2 lb cooked fish
1 oz butter
salt & pepper
egg & breadcrumbs

Take all skin and bone from fish and chop it finely, mash the potatoes with butter and mix altogether with seasonings, make into small round cakes on a floured board, brush with breadcrumbs, fry in hot dripping until nicely browned.

The Shrimpers of Paull

In the nineteenth century the small village of Paull on the River Humber bustled with activity as the local fishermen sold their trawl of shrimps to the visitors from Hull. Today the trade and the shrimpers have gone and most of us have to buy our shrimps from the frozen food department of a supermarket.

Stuffed Plaice

4 plaice fillets
10 oz shrimps or prawns
1 egg
2 tablespoons breadcrumbs
lemon juice
salt & pepper
parsley
1/2 pint shrimp or anchovy sauce

Place two of the plaice fillets in a greased ovenproof dish and squeeze over a little lemon juice, season with salt amd pepper. Chop 8 oz shrimps and place in bowl with breadcrumbs, lemon juice and egg and mix well. Place this stuffing on the fillets and put the other two fillets on top and press down gently. Cover with cooking foil and cook for no more than half an hour in a medium oven.

Make a basic white sauce using half milk and half fish or vegetable stock and simmered with a bay leaf; add the remaining shrimps just as the sauce is thickening or add 1 teaspoon anchovy essence. Drizzle a little sauce over the cooked plaice, decorate with parsley and serve the rest in a separate sauce boat.

Savoury Fish Custard

Mrs Daisy Hall, Filey

1/2 to 3/4 lb skinned cod/haddock fillets
1/2 pint milk
1 beaten egg
salt & pepper
lemon juice
parsley
garnish of lemon & olive

Cut fish into small pieces and place in ovenproof dish. Season with salt, pepper and lemon juice and leave to soak. Heat milk slightly and pour on to egg; spoon over fish. Sprinkle with chopped parsley and cook in moderate oven 40-45 minutes. When cooked garnish with lemon fan or sliced olives.

Today we can enjoy fresh fish frozen by modern methods in any season, likewise shellfish can be obtained at almost any time. In the old days, fish was eaten in season and along the East Coast, cod, halibut, herring and mackerel were caught by local fishermen and cooked the same day.

Herring Pie

Mrs Milner ,Whitby

4 fresh herrings, cleaned, boned and filleted
4 medium sized potatoes, sliced thinly
2 medium cooking apples, peeled and chopped
1 oz butter or margarine
salt and pepper
good handful of fresh parsley
juice of 1/2 lemon

Grease well a pie dish with the butter or margarine and line the base and sides with some of the potato slices, season with salt and pepper. Place the herring fillets, chopped apple, parsley and remaining potato slices in layers and squeeze the lemon juice, salt and pepper over each layer. Finish with a layer of sliced potato. Dot with butter or margarine. Cover with either a buttered paper or greased cooking foil and bake in a moderate oven for 30 minutes. Remove the cover and bake for a further 10 to 15 minutes to brown the top.

Potted Crab

Mrs Crossland, Leeds (Economical Recipes 1916)

1/2 lb picked crab
6 oz cooked haddock
salt & pepper
anchovy essence or sauce
ground mace to taste
2 oz melted butter.

Pound the crab and haddock together, add melted butter, season well. Press into pots and cover with melted butter.

Meat and Game

In 1894 a new teacher was employed by the Hull Municipal Technical School in Park Street, Hull. Miss Violet Freeborough came highly recommended, having been trained at the National Training School of Cookery, South Kensington. Her new position was in the Department of Women's Industries and she was to teach laundry and cookery in the kitchens of 7, Albion Street, Hull, to girls from local schools.

Miss Freeborough also taught the art of Middle-Class Cookery, the course of twelve lessons costing a fee of five shillings, and which would send young women out into the world prepared and ready for a life in service.

Unfortunately there are no records of the recipes that Miss Freeborough taught but the recipes given here from **Mrs A B Marshall's Cookery Book** *held at the Local History Unit, Hull College, are perhaps typical of the day.*

Ballotine of Pheasant with Cherry Salad

Take the leg of the pheasant and bone it; leave as much skin as possible to wrap over the farce; pound together half a pound of raw pheasant or any kind of game and a quarter of pound of raw ham or bacon and pass through a coarse wire sieve; season with a little corraline pepper, a pinch of salt, and add one large chopped truffle, four chopped button mushrooms, one ounce of cooked tongue or ham chopped, and mix with two raw yolks of eggs; force into the leg of the pheasant by means of a forcing bag and pipe. Make a little well in the centre of the farce with the finger wetted with warm water, and in the space put two ounces of pate de foie gras, which is cut into strips. Wrap the farce over and sew up the leg, tie up in a little buttered cloth and cook in good stock for rather better than half an hour. When cool cut in slices and mask with aspic mayonnaise and ornament with strips of tongue and French gherkin and little rounds of truffle in any pretty design; set the garnish with a little more aspic, trim the slices from the aspic, dish on a strip of aspic and garnish with cherry salad.

Little Chicken Cream

Take one pound of white meat, either veal, rabbit or chicken, scrape it and then pound it; mix it with half a pint of thick Bechamel sauce that has been tammied, a pinch of salt, a tiny dust of coralline pepper and one raw egg mixed up well together. Have some chicken moulds well buttered and sprinkled with a little chopped tongue or ham; then fill each mould with the prepared mixture; smooth them over with a wet warm knife, place them in a saute pan on a fold of paper and with a little boiling water in the bottom of the pan, and let them poach for about fifteen minutes in the oven with the cover on the pan; dish up on a border of potato or farce and garnish the centre with any nice green vegetables such as peas or macedoine, or points of asparagus, pour Veloute sauce over the little chickens and round the base of the dish and serve hot. The above quantity is sufficient for twelve little moulds.

Roast Haunch Venison

Take a haunch of venison which has been freed from the core and hung for fourteen to twenty one days, or even longer if liked, and which has been daily rubbed over with a dry cloth; saw off the knuckle and then rub all over with clean dripping and then wrap it up in a thickly greased paper; cover the paper over with a stiff cold water paste and then cover the paste all over with another greased paper, tie the haunch well over with string to keep the paste well together. Place the meat before a good clear fire or in a moderately heated oven and cook for four and a half to five hours, keeping well basted. Within half an hour of serving the venison, take it up and remove all paper and paste, dust the haunch well over with sifted flour and then put it again to the fire and let it get quite brown, keeping it basted. When ready to serve, dish it up and serve with a good clear gravy or brown sauce and have handed in a sauceboat some hot red currant jelly. Serve the venison very hot.

Deer once roamed freely on the great Yorkshire parks and estates, a rich man's sport and food for a poor man's family. The punishment for poaching venison in medieval times was dire, but today, happily, we can buy it from our butcher or game merchant with no fear of being put to the gallows or having our hands chopped off. Here is a recipe for today's cook with a suggestion of yesterday's pottage.

Casserole of Venison

2 lbs diced shoulder of venison
1 oz butter
2 tablespoons sunflower oil
1/2 pint red wine
1/2 pint stock
generous grating of nutmeg
4 cloves
1 stick of cinnamon
6 juniper berries
salt & freshly ground black pepper
seasoned flour
1 tablespoon redcurrant jelly

Dust the diced venison with the flour, heat the butter and oil in a large frying pan and quickly sear the meat all over. Remove from pan and put into a casserole dish. Pour the wine and the stock into the frying pan, stir into the remaining juices and simmer for about one minute, then pour over the venison. Add the spices including the pepper, but not the salt, cover with a well fitting lid and cook gently in a preheated, medium temperature oven for about 1 1/2 hours. Remove from oven, take out the cinnamon, add salt to taste and the redcurrant jelly and return to oven for another 15 minutes or until the meat is tender. Thicken if necessary with a tablespoon of arrowroot mixed with a little red wine or stock.

Braised Haunch of Venison

Joint of venison cut from the top of the haunch
4 strips of bacon or pork fat
2 onions sliced into rings
2 chopped carrots
2 stalks chopped celery
1 clove of chopped garlic
1 sprig of thyme
bunch of chopped parsley
2 bay leaves
1/2 pint red wine
2 tablespoons olive/sunflower oil
1/4 pint beef stock
1 tablespoon red wine vinegar
1 tablespoon brown sugar
6 black peppercorns
1 tablespoon redcurrant jelly

Preheat the oven to 350F 180C Gas Mark 4. Remove the skin from the venison and in a large pan brown the joint in the oil, then remove to a plate. Add the chopped vegetables, garlic and herbs to the oil in the pan, turn up the heat and stir for a few minutes, then transfer to a large casserole dish. Put the venison on top of the vegetables and lay the strips of fat over. Pour over the sugar, wine, peppercorns, vinegar and stock. Put on the lid and cook for approximately 2 hours. When tender, remove from casserole and place on heated meat plate. In another pan and over moderate heat, blend the flour with a little oil or butter, then gradually add the liquid from the casserole, first removing any excess fat and stir constantly until the sauce thickens. Add the redcurrant jelly and stir for one minute. Serve separately in a sauce boat.

I served the venison with creamed potatoes, roast parsnips, whole cooked chestnuts and sprouts, the parsnips and chestnuts complementing the sweetness of the redcurrant jelly in the sauce.

Every autumn a flock of pheasants escape from the shoot at nearby Burton Constable Hall Estate into the sanctuary of our garden. The cock birds are such a delight to watch, their iridescent feathers gleaming as they strut across the lawn with their bevy of buff coloured females following behind. One year, one bold fellow became quite tame and when I threw grain for our ducks he would tiptoe cautiously to join them at their supper. But in the eighteenth century, the throaty and evocative call of the plump wood pigeon, the heavy cacophonous flight of the pheasant or the white flash of a rabbit's tail would bring no sentimental smile to the face of Mrs Scryven or other country cooks, but would remind them that they had to prepare food for their master's table. Hare, rabbit, pigeon, partridge, pheasant or wild fowl flying over the estates on which they lived would be readily available. If pigeon isn't obtainable or to your taste, adapt this recipe and use rabbit or chicken pieces.

Mrs Scryven's Yorkshire Pye

8 rashers of bacon
2 pigeons chopped into 4 pieces
3 cups strong chicken stock (that will set to jelly)
pepper & salt
2 egg yolks beaten
4 tablespoons chopped parsley
2 tablespoons chopped lovage
2 bay leaves
4 shallots - chopped
8 ozs shortcrust or suet pastry

Line a casserole with the bacon, sprinkle in the shallots. Arrange the pigeon pieces and egg yolks on top, season, add the herbs and stock. Place a pie funnel in the centre and cover with a pastry lid. Cut a hole over the funnel. Flute the edges of the pastry and scratch the surface with a fork to make a ripple pattern. Glaze with egg wash and bake at 350 F. 180 C. Gas Mark 4 for 1 1/2 hours. Cover the lid with foil if it starts to burn. Insert a skewer through the pastry to check that the pigeon is tender.

As the early morning sun streaks the sky, the wild fowler waits up to his knees in cold river water for the beat of rapid wings and the dark cloud which, as it nears, reveals itself as the tight formation of long necked teal, widgeon and mallard gliding down to land and feed on the marshy river bank.

The meat of the wild duck has a different flavour from that of the domestic bird, more pronounced and 'gamey'; smaller and leaner it nevertheless requires a longer cooking time than the home reared bird. In the days of cooking over an open fire or range, the birds would be cooked on a spit with the juices dripping into a pan below, but today you can capture a similar flavour by oven roasting.

Wild Duck with Juniper and Thyme

2 oven ready Mallard or Teal
1 glass of port or red wine
1 teaspoon red wine vinegar
3 sprigs of Thyme
seasoned flour
melted butter
2 shallots or one onion
juniper berries
1 teaspoon arrowroot

Preheat the oven to 400F 200C or Gas Mark 6. Dust the ducks with seasoned flour and place one thyme sprig inside each. Make 2 small slits in each duck, one on each breast and insert 2 juniper berries. Dot each duck with butter and place on a rack in a roasting tin and roast for about one hour, basting frequently with melted butter and the juices.

Whilst the ducks are cooking, chop the shallots very fine and fry in a little olive or sunflower oil until golden; lower heat and add the port or wine and the remaining thyme sprig and simmer for 10 minutes.

Remove the ducks from the oven and place on a heated serving dish. Skim the fat from the roasting tin and add the sauce to the juices and stir; remove the sprig of thyme and add the red wine vinegar to sharpen the sauce. Thicken the sauce with arrowroot if needed. Spoon some of the sauce over the ducks to glaze and pour the rest into a warm sauce boat.

Serve with roast potatoes, brussels sprouts and thin slivers of braised carrots.

Stew and Dumplings

You may wonder why so commonplace a recipe as stew and dumplings is included in this book, for doesn't everyone know how to cook it? Well, so they might, but it is so easy to forget the traditional recipes when we are browsing in the supermarket and are confronted with a tempting array of food from other lands, of attractive packaging, fast food cooked in an instant in a microwave, or of a ready dinner simply popped into the oven to cook whilst we wait. Not that there is anything wrong with any of this, but the real pleasure in eating comes from having prepared the ingredients, of sniffing and tasting, of adding a little extra salt or pepper, a drop of wine to enhance and then relaxing as the aroma drifts from the kitchen and whets the taste buds in anticipation of what is to come.

2 lbs shin of beef or 3 lbs middle neck of lamb
1 onion
2 carrots
2 potatoes
1 small turnip or 2 parsnips
cooking oil
1 pint stock
1 cup wine, red for beef/white for lamb
2 sprigs marjoram/oregano
1 bay leaf
2 tablespoons fresh parsley
salt & pepper to taste
seasoned flour
1 clove garlic

Dumplings
4 ozs self raising flour
2 ozs grated suet
1/2 teaspoon salt
cold water to mix

Cut off excess fat from the meat, cube and coat in seasoned flour, chop into small cubes all the vegetables, crush the garlic and finely chop the herbs.

Heat a thin layer of oil in a frying pan and lightly sear the meat, vegetables and herbs (reserving one tablespoon of parsley), and turning them over with a spatula so that everything is coated.

Transfer to a deep, heavy pan or oven proof casserole with lid.

Pour half the stock and wine into the frying pan and bring to the boil, scraping all the residue from the meat and vegetables into it. Pour this over the meat and vegetables and then add the rest of the stock.

This can now either be cooked slowly in a moderate oven until the meat is tender or simmered on a hotplate or ring. When the meat is tender, add salt and pepper to your liking, raise the temperature with the lid off, and prepare the dumplings by mixing the flour, suet, salt and the remaining parsley in a bowl, adding sufficient cold water to make a stiff but pliable dough. Divide the dough into small balls and put into the near boiling stew. Cook for a further 15 minutes.

Beef and Pheasant Casserole

Raye Roberts, Cherry Burton

1 oven ready pheasant
1 lb braising steak/shin or skirt
2 tablespoons cooking oil
2 onions/shallots
2 tablespoons plain flour
1/2 pint red wine
3/4 pint beef stock
1 tablespoon red wine vinegar
1 teaspoon dried thyme
4 tablespoons cranberry sauce
4 oz button mushrooms

Joint the pheasant and cut each joint in half. Trim the fat off the meat and cut the meat into 1" cubes. Heat the oil in a saucepan until very hot and fry the pheasant pieces until well browned on all sides. Remove and place them in a large ovenproof casserole dish. Reheat the oil and fry the beef until brown. Add to the pheasant. Peel the onions and cut them into 8 pieces and fry for 5 minutes until golden. Sprinkle on the flour, stir and cook for 1-2 minutes. Stir in the wine, stock and vinegar. Season to taste, add the thyme and cranberry sauce. Pour over the meat in the casserole. Cover with a well fitting lid and cook for 2 hours, 350F. 180C. Gas Mark 4, until the meat is tender. Add the mushrooms, stir and cook for further 30 minutes.

Game Pie

1/2 hare
1 pheasant
1 partridge
2 pigeons
1/2 lb ham
1/2 lb mushrooms
1 quart good vegetable stock

Cut the hare and birds into joints, pack closely into stewpan or jar, add stock and cover closely; simmer gently for one hour. Lay the ham and mushrooms on top and simmer for one hour longer strain off the gravy, season well and set aside to cool and remove the fat. Take bones from the game and pack into a game pie mould with mushrooms and ham, finely chopped. Fill the mould with gravy and allow to cool. Garnish the top with parsley and sliced and quartered lemon. Serve as cold luncheon or supper dish.

Chicken & Parsley Pie

Cut some slices from the chicken (or veal). Season with salt. Scald some parsley and squeeze it dry. Cut it a little and lay at the bottom of dish. Then the meat and so on in layers. Fill the dish with new milk but not so high as to touch the crust. Cover it (with pastry) and when baked pour out a little of the milk and put in half a pint of cream.

Squab Pie

Mutton chops, onions, apples, sugar

Cut apples and lay them in rows with mutton chops. Shred onion and sprinkle among them and also some sugar.

Eel Pie

Cut the eels in lengths of 2 or 3 inches. Season with salt and pepper and place in dish with some bits of butter and a little water. Cover it with pastry.

Rabbit Pudding

Short pastry, 2 rabbits, ham or bacon
1 onion chopped very small, chopped parsley, salt and pepper

Line a greased pudding bowl with good pastry, 1/2" thick. Cut the rabbits into pieces, removing any sharp bone. Wash them well and drain on a clean cloth. Season with parsley, pepper and salt and onion. Add a few slices of ham or bacon. Cover with a lid of pastry, first wetting the edges and pressing down with the fingers. Tie the bowl in a cloth and immerse in a pan of boiling water and boil for two hours.

Yorkshire Pudding

Traditionally, Yorkshire Pudding was made in the same tin as the meat, beef or pork, had been roasted in, so that the flavour of the fat and the meat was absorbed into the batter. Today, some of us bake the pudding in patty tins instead. The choice is yours.

Most Yorkshire women (and some men), have their own special method, but for those who consider it a mystique and haven't yet made this most delicious of savoury puddings, here is the basic recipe; but before you try it, read first of all how the Pudding came to be.

Once upon a long time ago an Angel fell to earth, and he came down into a wild moorland district. He was quite, quite lost. He was cold and wet, his wings drooped and were bedraggled and he shivered greatly.

Through the darkness of the stormy day he saw a light and he stumbled towards it. The light was shining from the curtainless window of a poor hovel and inside the room he could see a woman preparing a meal.

He knocked on the door with his cold wet hand and the woman came to open it.

"By, lad!" she said, on seeing the soaking wet Angel. "What's tha doing out in weather like this? Come on in and warm thaself."

He sat down by the fire as she directed and soon he became warm and his wings dried out. "What place am I at?" he asked.

"Tha's in Yorkshire, lad. Can't tha tell?"

She set another place at the table and bid the Angel join her and her husband for their midday meal. "It's nowt much," she said, "we can't afford much meat, but there's plenty o' pudding and tha's welcome to share what we have."

The slices of meat were small but the pudding lay in a large tin in the middle of the table; it was pale in colour and very, very, solid, made substantially to feed hungry people.

The Angel looked at the pudding and then at the kind couple who had welcomed a stranger and offered to share their meagre meal with him. He stood up and stretched his wings, which were now dry, feathery and light; he fluttered them in that tiny room and touched the pudding with the tips.

"May your puddings always be as light as an Angel's wing," he said, in a voice that rang like a church bell, and as the woman and her husband watched in amazement, the pudding rose in the tin, light as a feather and crisp and golden.

"I've never tasted owt like it," said the husband, as gravy ran down his chin. "Never in my life!"

The Angel smiled a heavenly smile and took his leave of them. "That is how Yorkshire Pudding will always be, providing it is made with love and kindness."

There are many versions of this story, this one is mine!

Recipe

3oz strong white flour
1 egg
3 fluid ozs milk and water
pinch of salt
oil or fat for pudding tins

Put flower into large bowl, add egg, salt, milk and water and beat vigorously to a smooth batter with lots of air bubbles. Leave to stand (though this is not essential).

Put a small knob of fat or 1/2 teaspoon of oil into the pudding tins and place in hot oven until smoking. Add batter and bake until well risen and golden with crisp brown edges. In small patty tins these will take about 15/20 minutes. In a large meat tin it takes a little longer.

Serve as an accompaniment to Roast Beef, Roast Pork or Lamb, with onion gravy.

Don't You Know There's A War On?

During the Great War of 1914/18 economy was encouraged and during the second World War of 1940/45 the population of Great Britain were urged to 'Tighten your belts' and to 'Dig for Victory' for the War Effort; and when the question, 'What's for dinner?' was asked, the answer was often, 'Pot Luck'!

Food rationing was announced in 1940 and was to continue into the 1950's. 2oz butter, 4oz margarine, 8oz sugar, 4oz cheese and 2oz of tea were allowed per person per week and one egg each fortnight. But housewives and cooks were both practical and adept, none more so than those from Yorkshire, and as the days of cooking with rich cream, butter and eggs diminished and food from abroad disappeared from the shelves, they became expert at making a little go a long way in those utilitarian years.

They substituted strips of carrot for orange peel, they used dried egg, adapted recipes and named them 'Mock' or 'Imitation'. They made jam from carrots and cooked stews in hay boxes to save fuel; they planted vegetables in their flower beds and kept hens in their back yards.

The Ministry of Food in 1940 urged everyone to cook potatoes in their skins and to eat plenty of vegetables and salad for a healthy life, and sent out instructors from 'The Kitchen Front' to teach economy in the kitchen and make the most of the food rations.

Here are some of those recipes from both periods, which in some instances are still in use today.

Economical Dinners
S.J.C. 1916

Make a good suet crust, roll out and spread with minced cold meat, season with salt and pepper, one onion if liked, roll up, tie in a cloth and boil for 1 1/2 hours or according to size. This served with a dish of parsnips or other vegetables and potatoes, with gravy and sauce, makes a good dinner.

Stuffed Marrow
Mrs Shaw (Economical Recipes 1916) Driffield

Cut a vegetable marrow in half lengthways, remove the seeds. Mince any kind of cold meat, dredge over it with a little flour, pepper, salt and minced onion. Bind all together with the yolk of an egg or a little stock and fill the marrow with this mixture. Tie the two halves together and stew it in some well flavoured stock. When the marrow is soft, remove it, and thicken (the stock) with a little flour. Pour over the marrow and serve hot.

To Make Bacon go Further
Mrs Hopper (Economical Recipes 1916) Driffield

Soak all odd pieces of stale bread in a little water, then squeeze as dry as possible and rub through grater into a basin. Add three ozs of chopped suet, one cupful of flour, one small chopped onion, a little chopped parsley, thyme, salt and pepper. Mix well together, then tie tightly in a cloth and boil for two hours. When cold, cut into little rounds and fry in bacon fat. This has the delicious flavour of bacon and is very nourishing; also only half the usual quantity of bacon need be fried to go with this.

When sending to your boy in the trenches, include in your parcel a penny mustard tin with a small piece of sandpaper glued to the outside. This makes a safety match-box.
Mr F Johnson 1916

And the soldier in the trenches still retained his sense of humour when he sent home this recipe to be included in Economical Recipes:

Trench Pudding
A soldier friend 1916

Take two army biscuits and pound them well with a hammer, put them to steep overnight, and a few currants if you are lucky enough to have any. Put the lot in a mess tin and cook over a candle wrapped with a cloth to give more heat. Cost one penny.

And he would no doubt be glad of the tip that;
A few drops of paraffin added to boot polish will enable you to give quite a good shine to damp boots.

Delicious Pork Brawn
Miss F Wiles (Economical Recipes 1916) Driffield

Procure threepennyworth of pork bones and rinds from your butcher, boil for 2 1/2 hours, take up, remove the meat from the bones, put with the rinds and chop up all together moderately small, season well with pepper and salt, put into a large basin with some of the liquor, and when cold turn out. You will have one and a half pounds of delicious brawn. The remaining stock can be used up for soup or gravies.

The first day of war,
September 4th 1939.

"The task will be hard," said the King. "There may be dark days ahead —."

Petrol was to be rationed and more land put to the plough.

Can you answer YES to these questions?

Have you signed your name on your new Identity Card?

Have you cut out your Clothing Book from your Food Ration Book and filled in your name and address on the front cover?

Have you filled in your address on the front cover of your Food Ration Book, filled in page 35, Section A, and made sure that page 36 has been properly filled in?

Have you filled in your name and National Registration number on any Personal Points sheet which you have taken out of the book?

If not, see that you do them all at once.

To Make a Hay Box

Line a biscuit tin, bottom and sides with thick newspaper. Place hay or straw in box round the sides and bottom. Bring your stew or porridge to simmer point and place in hay box with its lid firmly in place. Put more hay on top and a wad of newspaper, with the biscuit tin lid on. Your dinner will be ready when you have done your war work.

To use Processed Egg

To equal 1 egg; 1/2 oz powder - good weight, 3 tablespoons cold water. Mix the powder to a paste with a little of the water, pressing out all the lumps, add the rest of the water gradually. Soak overnight if possible. Remember that dried eggs are simply whole new laid eggs with nothing taken away except the water and the shell.

Dalton Pie
Maureen Kirk, Hull

Any vegetable you have in store plus 1/2 lb sausages, pastry to cover. Cut up vegetables and onions into bite size pieces and steam. Fry the sausages and cut into one inch pieces. Place vegetables and sausages into a pie dish and cover with a little gravy. Top with gravy made by adding a little mustard to flour and liquid paraffin. Bake in a hot oven. Instead of sausages, corned beef cut up into cubes can be used instead.

Medley Pie
Mr Thomas

Take enough bacon to line a pie dish, cover with sliced onions and sprinkle over one dessertspoon of sage. Add salt and pepper. Cover with a good layer of apples, pared and quartered and sweeten to taste. Add half a teacup of water and cover the whole with a good short crust pastry. Bake in a moderate oven until nicely brown.

Jugged Hare
Mrs Flo Hirst

Have ready some good stock strongly flavoured with onion. After cutting up the hare put it in an earthenware jar (wide mouthed). Pour the stock over the hare entirely covering it, and throw in 6 cloves and 2 bay leaves, one inch stick of cinnamon, the juice of 1/2 lemon, a little pepper and salt and little piece of lemon rind about an inch, and all the blood of the hare; if the stock has not been flavoured with onion cut up an onion and add it. Then put on the lid of the jar and place in a pan of boiling water. It will require cooking for 2 1/2 hours.

The jar should not be packed but have plenty of room for the gravy to get between the pieces of hare. Serve with forcemeat balls and place them round the dish.

Serve the gravy thick by lathering with flour 20 minutes before serving. Also serve Red Currant Jelly.

Imitation Jugged Hare
E.S.

Take 2 lbs shin of beef, cut it in pieces as large as the joints of the hare, flour them and fry them a nice brown in dripping. Now put them in a casserole or stew pan, add to them an onion, a strip of lemon rind, a teaspoon of mixed spice, pepper and salt to taste, pour over enough hot water or stock to cover, then cover the vessel closely and cook gently for 3 hours. Put the meat in a hot tureen, thicken the gravy, then add a teaspoon of vinegar or ketchup. If served with redcurrant jelly and forcemeat balls, it is delicious.

38

Maureen Kirk of Hull wrote to tell me of some of the things she and her family used to do during the last war; she calls it 'Dispatches from the Home Front'. Nothing was ever wasted; tea, left over in the pot made good gravy, and her grandmother always combed cold tea through her hair to cover the grey! They used liquid paraffin instead of lard or margarine to make pastry, and young women coloured their legs with permanganate of potash when they couldn't buy stockings. They then used a black pencil to draw a line up the back of their legs, and, said Maureen, the chaps didn't complain!

Mock Crab
Mr Fox

1 oz grated cheese
1/2 oz butter
1 teaspoon anchovy essence
1 teaspoon vinegar
1/2 teaspoon made mustard
a little pepper

Warm the butter and mix all well together. Can be used on buttered toast or filling for hard boiled eggs or sandwiches.

Mary's Mock Crab
Mrs Alice Brindley

3 large tomatoes
1 onion
1 egg
2 ozs grated cheese
4 ozs dry breadcrumbs
1 oz margarine
pepper & salt

Skin and chop tomatoes, grate onion, melt fat and cook until soft. Add beaten egg, beating all smoothly and stir until it thickens. Take off heat and add cheese and breadcrumbs, put into pots and cover with melted butter.

Savoury Pie
Mrs Markham

Good short pastry
1 lb pig's fry
1/2 lb lean pork
2 onions
2 dessertspoons flour
salt & pepper, sage

Line a baking dish with a good layer of pastry. Cut up the pig's fry and pork and toss well in seasoned flour. Add pepper and salt. Peel the onions and cut them into rings, add chopped sage to taste. Mix well together and put into the pastry lined dish. Add water or stock to cover and bake in a moderate oven for 1 1/2 hours, taking care that the pastry doesn't burn. Serve with apple sauce and mashed potatoes.

Mock Goose

2 lb mashed potatoes
1 lb onions, boiled until tender
1 lb sausage meat
a little thyme and sage added to the boiled onions
dripping

Take a deep dish and grease it with dripping. Then put in layers of mashed potatoes, sausage meat and boiled onions. Continue until the dish is full. The last layer should be potatoes. Put a little dripping on top and bake half an hour in a moderate oven. This makes an inexpensive dinner, said the unknown cook.

Penny Ducks

Penny Ducks, Savoury Ducks or Faggots are just three of the names given to describe this wartime savoury dish which was made from offal, breadcrumbs and suet, formed into small balls or flat cakes, wrapped in pig's apron or kell (membrane), and fried. They are still sold today in butcher's shops and delicatessens.

1/4 lb breadcrumbs
1/4 lb chopped pig's liver
1/4 lb onions, chopped fine
1/4 lb suet
1 tablespoon chopped sage
salt & pepper
1 egg beaten

Put all ingredients together in a bowl and mix well. Form into flat cakes and fry in dripping or oil until golden brown on both sides.

And for a cheap nourishing dish served with creamy mashed potatoes and thick slices of bread to dip, what better than;

Tripe and Onions

1 lb tripe
2 large onions
salt and pepper
1 oz flour
1/2 pint milk

Put tripe into a large saucepan and cover with cold water, bring to boil, then strain. Cut the tripe into small pieces and return to pan with chopped onions. Cover with hot water and simmer until tripe is tender. Mix flour and cold milk to a paste and add to liquor in pan, reheat until it thickens. Add seasoning to taste.

Tinned Corned Beef Hash
Mr Sherry, Hull

8 oz corned beef
4 oz haricot beans soaked overnight
2 dessertspoons pearl barley
1 crushed beef cube
2 chopped onions
1 sliced carrot
2 oz turnip or swede cut into small cubes
1 bay leaf or sprig of mint
salt and pepper

Rinse the beans and place in pan along with other ingredients except the corned beef. Well cover them with heated stock or boiling water and boil slowly until the beans are cooked, stir occasionally. Then add the beef cut into small pieces and thicken the hash with a little flour and heat through.

Toad in the Hole

2 ozs beef dripping or 2 tablespoons sunflower oil
5 ozs flour
2 eggs
1/2 pint milk
1 lb beef steak cut into strips
salt & pepper

Put the dripping or oil into a roasting tin. Put flour, eggs and milk into a bowl and beat well. Put a quarter of this batter into the roasting tin and cook at 400 F. 200 C. Gas Mark 6 until lightly set. Season the beef and lay on top of the batter and cover with the rest of the batter. Bake for 40 minutes until well risen and golden.

When I was a child during the war, my granny cooked ham and bacon for my uncle who kept a grocery shop in Castleford market hall. She would rise early and fill her copper — or 'set pot' with water, light the fire beneath it and put the bacon in to boil. When it was cooked she used to cut off a thick slice, presumably as payment for her effort. I haven't tasted ham or bacon like it since, but I do wonder what today's environmental health officers would have to say about the cooking methods employed below!

Cooking a Ham
An Economical Method Sent by Mr Sherry

Put your ham in the copper, well cover with cold water and slowly bring to the boil. Boil for twenty minutes if ham is 15 lbs or under, for 20 lbs or more one hour is sufficient. Then take away all the fire from underneath and well cover the copper with old coats, bags or anything to keep in the heat. Leave for about 12 hours. Lift off coats, cover etc, and if ham is cold enough lift ham on dish. You will have a well cooked but not over cooked ham with a minimum amount of fuel.

Honey Glazed York Ham

York ham is cured with dry salt, lightly smoked and matured for several months. It is a very popular ham due to its mild and tender flavour. The size can vary from 12 pounds upwards and so is usually sold at Christmas. This recipe parboils the joint and then honey roasts in the oven. Timing is worked out at 25 minutes to the pound but can vary according to the curing of the ham.

Soak the ham overnight or as long as possible to remove excess salt, then place into a large pan, cover with fresh cold water and bring slowly to the boil. Cover with a lid, reduce heat and cook at low simmering point for 2 hours (for a 12 lb ham).

Turn off heat and remove the joint from the pan. Wrap closely in cooking foil, place in a roasting tin and cook in the centre of preheated oven 350 F. 180 C. Gas Mark 4 for approx 2 1/2 to 3 hours.

Remove from oven, remove foil and peel off skin. Score a diamond pattern in the exposed fat, stud with cloves and drizzle honey over the top of the joint to glaze. Return to hot oven for further 1/2 hour to crisp and finish.

Puddings

Every year in late summer or autumn, I put on an old long sleeved shirt and thick skirt or trousers and go 'brambling' in the wild part of our garden. Sometimes my mother or daughters or grandson go with me. Mother puts on her straw hat and takes a stool to sit on and in easy companionship we pick the juicy black fruit and plan what we shall make; shall it be a simple crumble, served with thick golden custard or cream? Shall it be a creamy Bramble Fool, or a gallon of heady Bramble Wine? Or shall we freeze some and save for cold winter days when the taste and flavour serves to remind us of the summer just past?

Bramble and Apple Crumble

1/2 lb ripe brambles cleaned and de-stalked
3 large cooking apples, sliced
4 ozs sugar

Topping
6 ozs self raising flour
2 ozs porridge oats
2 ozs sugar
4 ozs margarine

Grease a deep dish and layer apples and brambles into it. Sprinkle with sugar. Put flour, oats, fat and sugar in a bowl and mix together with your fingers, then cover the fruit in the dish. Dot with margarine and a sprinkling of oats to make the topping crunchy.

Cook in a medium hot oven until the topping starts to turn golden brown. Serve hot with custard, cream, or vanilla ice cream.

Yorkshire Apple Pudding

1/2 lb self raising flour
2 eggs
1 pint milk
pinch salt
2 large baking apples
2 tablespoons cooking oil
2 ozs sugar

Sift flour, salt and sugar into a basin, break in the eggs add half the milk and stir until smooth. Add the rest of the milk and beat well. Peel the apples, grate them into the mixture and stir. Pour the oil into a pudding tin and heat in oven until hot. Pour in apple batter and bake in a hot oven for about 40 minutes until well risen and crisp at the edges. Serve sprinkled with sugar and a topping of cream.

Apple Charlotte
Book of Recipes 1907

Well butter a pie dish and place a good layer of breadcrumbs on the bottom, put dabs of butter here and there among the crumbs. Fill up the dish with sliced apples, cover well with sugar and then place another layer of crumbs and butter. On the top put the apple parings and cook in a moderate oven for 45 minutes. Take off the parings, turn out on a hot dish, cover with fine sugar and serve with cream.

I have been given many recipes for Railway Pudding, but no explanation as to why it was so named. This first recipe was sent to me by Mr Prior, a former Huddersfield man who inherited his grandmother's recipe book. Inside the book were photographs of his grandmother, Mrs Flo Hirst, and her family on a picnic in 1914. The ladies sat elegantly on the grass in long dresses or two piece 'costumes' and they all wore large hats with trailing or plumed feathers. One small boy wore his school cap whilst another older boy sported a straw boater.

Railway Pudding
Mrs F Hirst

Put some jam at the bottom of a pie dish then half fill with breadcrumbs, a custard, made of milk, 2 eggs and sugar placed over. Bake 1/2 an hour. Turn out of the pie dish. Eat hot or cold.

Railway Pudding
Mrs Walgate (Economical Recipes) 1916

Work 2 oz butter to a cream, then add 1 cup of sugar and 1 egg. Beat well. Add 1 cup of flour and just before putting in the oven, mix in 1 teaspoon baking powder. Bake in a well greased dripping tin and when ready, spread with jam and roll. Serve cold or hot with custard.

Mary's Ginger Pudding

Mr D Thomas, Halifax

1/2 lb flour
1/4 lb suet
1/4 lb treacle
2 teaspoons ground ginger
1/2 teaspoon bicarbonate soda
1 teacup warm milk

Mix dry ingredients together, dissolve bicarbonate of soda in warm milk. Mix all and pour into greased mould. Cover over top with greased paper and steam for three hours.

Treacle Pudding

Mrs A Ambler, Castleford

4oz self raising flour
4oz breadcrumbs
4oz shredded suet
4 tablespoons treacle (golden syrup)
1 egg
rind and juice of 1 lemon

Mix together flour, breadcrumbs, suet, treacle, and grated lemon rind. Add beaten egg until a good consistency, add lemon juice and mix well.

Steam in well buttered basin for 2 hours or bake in medium hot oven for about 3/4 hour or until well risen or golden.

Fruit Fools have been made since the late eighteenth century: any soft fruit can be used, the slender pink stems of young rhubarb, ripe gooseberries, raspberries or bramble. Some are made with custard, some with cream, some with egg white. Here are two very old recipes.

Fruit Cream.

Recipe Ann Miller. 1845

1 Cup cleaned Raspberries
2 1/2 cups cleaned Red or Blackcurrants
1/4 lb caster sugar
1 pint cream

Cook the fruit for 15 minutes. Cool then add sugar and cream, stirring constantly. Serve in a glass dish so that the colour shows through.

Fruit Fool.

1 lb Gooseberries
2 tablespoons rosewater
6 ozs sugar
4 egg whites, whipped.

Top and tail gooseberries. Cook them in a little water until soft, cool and drain off liquid. Rub them through a strainer and return to pan with rosewater and sugar. Whisk the egg whites until frothy and stir into gooseberries over a gentle heat until the mixture thickens. Cool and serve in glasses.

My Fruit Fool.

1/2 lb gooseberries or other soft fruit
(cleaned or topped and tailed)
1 pint of cooled custard
6 ozs sugar/ or to taste
dollop of soft vanilla icecream

Cook the fruit until soft, adding sugar gradually until it melts.When cool whizz in a blender or push through a sieve to make a puree. Put into a large bowl, add the cooled custard and mix well, transfer to a glass bowl, add icecream and stir gently so that the icecream streaks through the custard.

Syllabub

Syllabub was originally a rich drink with milk fresh from the cow, with added cream and a frothing wine. Later, brandy or sherry, eggs and sugar were added to make an even richer dessert. Today it is sometimes used as a topping for trifles or jellies, but it is at its best served on its own as a dessert in tall glasses at the end of a meal.

2 tablespoons of white wine
1 tablespoon brandy or sherry
juice of 1/2 lemon
1 oz caster sugar
1/2 pint double cream
2 egg whites, stiffly beaten

Put the wine, brandy, sugar and lemon juice together in a large bowl and stir occasionally until the sugar dissolves. Add the cream and whisk until it stands in peaks. Stir in the beaten egg whites and gently whisk again. Keep cool until ready to serve.

Frumatty

Or Frumenty, is an old yeoman farmers' dish and in the country district of Holderness in the East Riding, it was traditionally 'set on 'table' on Christmas Eve in a large bowl, and along with spice cake, mincepies, mulled wine or punch was offered to any visitors who might chance to call.

Simmer enough kibbled wheat (crushed wheat) for 12 hours; then add a nut of butter, mixed spice, currants or sultanas, sugar, rum and cream and stir.

Granny's Bread and Butter Pudding.

Two or three years ago I invited some friends over for supper and asked which they would prefer, a lavish dessert or bread and butter pudding? Without exception, up shot their hands like the school children they had been when last tasting this most delicious of puddings. The verdict was unanimous; it still tasted as good as ever! Currently it is very much back in favour, and deservedly so.

6 thick slices of white bread
2 ozs butter or low fat spread
2 ozs currants or sultanas
2 ozs sugar
2 eggs
1 pint milk
Nutmeg

Remove crusts from bread and spread with butter or low fat spread and cut into squares. Put half of the squares into a well greased oven dish. Sprinkle with all the fruit and half the sugar. Top with remaining bread, buttered side up and sprinkle with rest of the sugar. Beat the eggs and milk together and pour over bread mixture. Leave to stand for at least half an hour so that the bread absorbs most of the liquid. Sprinkle with nutmeg and bake in the centre of a moderate oven 325 F.163 C. or Gas No 3 for about 1 hour or until the pudding is set and the top crisp and golden.

When I was a child my family used to spend our summer holidays in Scarborough, staying with grandparents and spending our days in a holiday chalet in the North Bay, right on the edge of the beach. The days were always sunny, the sands soft and golden and the sea invigorating. With our cousins we hunted for crabs in the rock pools, had birthday parties on the sands, learned to dance at the Tea Dances in the Corner Cafe and ate slices of;

Aunt Edna's Apple Pie

Mrs E Ware

4 oz self raising flour
4 oz plain flour
2 oz lard
2 oz margarine
1 lb Bramley apples
4 oz sugar
1 tablespoon lemonade
cinnamon (optional)

Slice the Bramleys and cook gently in a pan with the lemonade for 3 or 4 minutes, then remove from heat. Sieve both flours together, rub in the fats and add sufficient cold water to make a good pastry. Chill before rolling out. Cut pastry into 2 equal pieces, roll out one of the pieces and use to line a greased pie plate. Cover pastry with layers of apple, sprinkling each layer with sugar and cinnamon if used. Moisten the edges of pastry with water and roll out second piece of pastry to make lid. Press edges well together and make slit in the middle. Flake edges of pie with the back of a knife or the prongs of a fork and decorate with pastry leaves. Brush with beaten egg or milk and sprinkle with caster sugar. Stand pie on baking tray and bake in centre of hot oven for about 20 minutes. Reduce heat to moderate and bake for further 20 minutes, making sure that the underside of pie is cooked. Remove from oven when ready and whilst still hot sprinkle with a little more caster sugar. Aunt Edna used to serve this 'lemony' apple pie with fresh cream, but it is equally as good with hot custard or icecream or eaten cold with a slice of Wensleydale cheese.

Apple and Orange Tart, 1594

2 oranges
5 medium apples
2 tablespoons flour
6 ozs sugar
1 teaspoon cinnamon
1/2 teaspoon ginger
1/2 oz butter
1 1/2 lb short pastry

Peel, core and slice the apples. Peel the oranges and divide into segments. Combine both fruits in a bowl and toss with the flour, sugar and spices. Pile into a dish lined with pastry, dot the fruit with butter and cover with rest of pastry. Sprinkle with sugar. Bake in a medium hot oven for 40 minutes.

Cakes

Several of the old recipes and books I have been given or loaned, contained recipes which were the same or similar to each other, proving therefore that these were tried and tested favourites. Many of the cake recipes contained orange and walnut, and ginger was used constantly, in gingerbread, parkin, cakes, snaps, biscuits and brandysnap. Some recipes, particularly in the very old personal books, gave the ingredients only and not the instructions on making, which assumed, I thought, that most women in those days would know how to mix a cake or make and bake a 'good' pastry. Most too, advised, not on temperature control but whether a hot, medium or cool oven was required. Many of the recipes were designated as 'Auntie's Cake', or 'Mother's Cake', or 'Mrs Such and Such's Recipe'. In as many instances as possible I have presented the recipes as originally worded, for this, I felt, added to their charm as the faraway voices of those long ago cooks echo back through the years.

1-2-3-4 Cake
Mrs Danby (Economical Recipes 1916)

1 teacupful of butter, 2 of sugar, 3 of flour, 4 eggs. 1 teaspoon baking powder and 1/2 teacup milk.
Fruit or seed can be added if liked.

Seed Loaf, 1907

6 oz butter
6 oz lard
1 lb fine sugar
1/4 candied peel
2 lb flour
4 teaspoons baking powder
6 eggs
1 teaspoon caraway seed

Beat the butter and lard to a cream, add the sugar and candied peel well chopped, then the eggs and lastly the flour, powder and seeds.

Orange Cake

3 eggs, their weight in fine sugar, butter and flour, the grated rind and juice of a sweet orange, 1 small teaspoon of baking powder.

Beat the butter and sugar to a cream, add the eggs which should have been well beaten beforehand, add half the flour, beating well for some time, then the rind and juice of the orange, add the remainder of the flour and the baking powder, continue beating for five minutes, pour into a well greased sandwich cake tin and bake in a moderate oven half an hour.

48

Walnut Cake

2 eggs
1/4 lb butter
1/4 lb sugar
1/4 lb flour
1 small teaspoon baking powder

Beat sugar and butter to a cream, beat eggs well, add them to butter and sugar beating all the time, then the flour and lastly the baking powder. Bake in a moderate oven about twenty minutes. When cold split and fill wth apricot jam and coat with vanilla icing, for which use 2 oz butter, 5 oz icing sugar and a little vanilla flavouring. Beat butter well, add sifted icing sugar and flavouring, spread on cake and cover with chopped walnuts.

Wartime Cake

Mrs Ball, Sproatley

2 cups any fruit
1 cup sugar
1 cup water
Boil all together and cool
2 heaped cups flour
2 ozs fat
1 teaspoon baking powder
1/2 teaspoon bicarbonate soda
pinch salt

Rub fat into flour (mix all together) and bake in moderate oven 1 1/2 hours. If liked, added Mrs Ball, dried egg, nutmeg and essence can be added, and treacle.

Custard Tart

Short pastry
2 eggs
1/2 pint milk
1 dessertspoon sugar

Line a pie dish with pastry. Beat eggs with milk and add sugar. Pour into the pastry and sprinkle with nutmeg. Bake in a hot oven until set.

Ground Rice Cheese Cakes, 1907

2 oz ground rice, 2 oz butter, 2 oz sugar, 1 egg, raspberry jam.

Beat the butter to a cream, add the sugar, egg and ground rice. Line small patty tins with either flaky or short pastry, put a little jam in each, then a teaspoon of the mixture. Bake in a quick oven for twenty minutes.

Edith Gibson's little black book, kindly lent to me by Mrs Gertude Attwood, contains many recipes for Yorkshire Parkin. There's Stoodly View Parkin, Mrs Greenwood's Parkin, Moggy Parkin and Treacle Parkin. Parkin was a very old favourite, particularly in the West Riding of Yorkshire, a standard item kept in a tin in practically every larder, ready to offer any casual caller. This recipe is an amalgamation of all four, tried and tasted.

Yorkshire Parkin

1/2 lb S/R Flour
1/4 lb medium oatmeal
3 ozs sugar
2 teaspoons ground ginger
5 tablespoons golden syrup
6 ozs margarine
1 egg
1 tablespoon black treacle

Mix all dry ingredients. Melt syrup and fat in pan and pour on to dry ingredients. Mix well, then add beaten egg. Pour into a deep greased tin 8"x10" and bake in a slow oven 350F 180C Gas Mark 4 until golden brown.

Parkin Pigs

Mrs Binns, Halifax

8 ozs self raising flour
4 ozs sugar
3 ozs margarine or lard
1 tablespoon syrup
1 teaspoon bicarbonate soda
1 teaspoon ginger
1 tablespoon boiling water

Rub fat into flour, add sugar and ginger. Mix bicarbonate of soda with boiling water and add with the syrup to the dry ingredients, mix to a stiff paste, roll out and cut with a biscuit cutter. Bake in a medium oven until golden.

Ginger Cake

Mrs Gertrude Attwood, Hull

4 oz margarine or butter
4 oz soft brown sugar
1 egg
1/2 lb self raising flour
1 level teaspoon bicarbonate soda
2 good level teaspoons ground ginger
1/8 pint milk
1 generous tablespoon of golden syrup

Cream margarine and sugar and stir in the egg with a tablespoon of flour, then add rest of flour, bicarbonate of soda and ground ginger and mix well. Gently heat golden syrup and milk, pour into the other ingredients and mix well, adding a drop more warm milk if necessary to make a 'sloppy' mixture which will pour easily into a greased and lined 2 lb loaf tin. Bake in the upper part of oven at 325 F.170C. Gas Mark 3 for 1/2 hour, then reduce to 300 F.150C. Gas Mark 2 and put cake on lower shelf for further 1/4 hour.

No Egg Ginger Cake

This recipe for a 'no egg cake' was used regularly during the last war when eggs were scarce. Mrs Barker told me that this cake keeps really well and after a couple of days becomes very moist and sticky. I tried it and it does!

Mrs J Barker, Hedon

3 cups self raising flour
1 cup sugar
2 teaspoon ground ginger
1/4 lb margarine
1 cup golden syrup
1 cup boiling water

Mix flour, sugar and ginger and rub in margarine. Add golden syrup and boiling water and mix well until smooth. Pour into a greased and lined 8" square tin and bake for 1 1/4 to1 1/2 hours in the lower half of a moderate oven.

Mrs Newcombe's Ginger Oats

Mrs Allenby, Malton

1 1/2 cups of porridge oats
1 1/2 cups of sugar
1 1/2 cups plain flour
2 level teaspoons ground ginger
1 1/2 level teaspoons bicarbonate soda
4 oz margarine
1 tablespoon golden syrup
1 tablespoon hot water
flaked almonds

Dissolve the margarine and syrup in hot water. Mix together the dry ingredients and add to the margarine and syrup mixture, mix well. Form into pieces the size of walnuts and place onto a greased baking sheet. Flatten tops and place piece of flaked almond in middle. Bake in a moderate oven until golden brown.

Yorkshire Fruit Loaf

Yorkshire food travels well. Mrs Ethel Hardiman, formerly of Hessle, took this recipe for a fruit loaf with her to Toronto in Canada over thirty years ago, where she still makes it today.

8 oz flour
4 oz soft margarine
4 oz sugar
2 eggs
12 oz mixed fruit
1 teaspoon mixed spice
1 teaspoon baking powder
approx 1/4 pint milk

Mix all dry ingredients together, then add margarine, eggs and milk and mix well. Put into well greased and lined cake tin and place halved walnuts on top. Bake in the centre of a moderate oven for 1 1/2 hours.

Yorkshire Cheese Cake

Or Crud-Chuzzack or Chiskeeak, as Norman Stockton of the East Riding Dialect Society would call it, is an old favourite all over Yorkshire. It is baked golden with eggs and cream and butter and bursting with moist succulent fruit, and is snatched by eager hands when it appears on cake stalls at every village fete or Christmas Fair. There have been few variations over the years but the one given here is the standard Yorkshire recipe still in use today. If curd cheese is not available, cottage cheese can be used as long as it is well sieved and drained.

4 oz shortcrust pastry
8 oz curd cheese
2 eggs well beaten
2 oz caster sugar
grated rind of 1/2 lemon
juice of 1 lemon
2 teaspoons cornflour
2 tablespoons cream
1 tablespoon melted butter
2 oz raisins/sultanas or currants
grated nutmeg to taste

Grease a nine inch loose based tin and line with the pastry. Blend the cheese with the sugar, beaten eggs, lemon rind and juice. Beat until smooth, gradually adding the cornflour, cream and melted butter. Finally, gently fold in the fruit, sprinkle with grated nutmeg and pour the mixture into the pastry case. Bake in a preheated oven 350 F. 180 C. Gas Mark 4, for about 35/40 minutes.

In the autumn we are often knee deep in apples and as we enter the house there is a sweet and sour cidery aroma of apples just on the turn. We make wine, pies, crumbles, jams and jellies, and one year my mother came up with this recipe for;

Sproatley Apple Cake

2/3 large cooking apples, peeled and grated
8 ozs self raising flour
8 ozs sugar
4 ozs margarine
1/2 teaspoon baking powder
1 teaspoon mixed spice
2 eggs
6 ozs currants
6 ozs sultanas
2 ozs candied peel

Beat together sugar and margarine, gradually add flour, baking powder and eggs and mix until smooth, add mixed fruit, spice and apple and mix well. Turn into well greased cake tin and bake for 1 1/2 hours at 360 F 180 C Gas Mark 4. When cool, dredge with caster sugar.

Fruit Slice

Mrs D Harper, Sproatley
8 oz self raising flour
4 oz margarine
4 oz sugar
4 oz sultanas
2 oz mixed peel
1 teaspoon mixed spice
1 large egg beaten in a cup of milk

Rub flour and margarine together, add dry ingredients and mix well together with egg and milk. Pour into greased shallow baking tray and cook for 30 minutes at 350F 180C Gas Mark 4.

Afternoon Tea Scones

12 oz self raising flour
2 oz margarine
2 oz lard
2 oz sugar
2 oz currants
1 egg
1/2 teaspoon salt
milk

Put flour and salt into a bowl, rub in margarine and lard, add currants and sugar. Mix well. Beat egg and add it to dry ingredients with sufficient milk to make a spongy dough. Turn the mixture onto a floured board and roll out to 1/2 inch thickness. Cut into rounds, put onto a floured baking tray and bake in a quick oven for about 20 minutes.

It was a crisp, sunny, October morning when Catherine and I set out from the small market town of Hawes in Wensleydale; our aim to reach Hardraw Force, considered to be the most spectacular waterfall in the National Park. Our route took us along the river Ure, over the twin-arched New Bridge, keeping in view the heights of Stags Fell and across the sloping meadows towards the old villages of Sedbusk and Simonstone.

As we paused to take a breath we looked across the hillsides to where lime kilns, quarries and lead mines would once have been throbbing with activity, and where now only the hummocky meadows gave an indication of where they had been.

In the meadows, sheep were quietly grazing and the trees were rich in autumn colour; small wonder that Wordsworth and Turner were inspired by such beauty. Hardraw Force leapt in a cascading, sparkling silver ribbon and fell in a wedding veil pool of frothy white, and I was reminded of the Victorian ladies in their long gowns who walked along the scenic paths to admire the view.

Our return took us through kissing gates and the oh — so narrow Dales stiles set into the dry stone walls and onto part of the Pennine Way, and down once more towards Hawes and a most welcome pot of tea. This we found on a corner of the main street, in the Tea Tree Tea Rooms where there were so many tempting things to eat it was hard to make a decision, and as an extra compulsion for a bookworm like me, there is also an old bookshop to browse in.

Carolyn Boardman who owns the tea room does her own cooking and baking, nothing out of a packet, all good wholesome food, and after much deliberation we decided to try her Carrot Cake. This was so delicious that I plucked up the courage to ask her if she would be willing to share her recipe. Generously she said that she would, and here it is.

Carolyn's Carrot Cake

9 ozs soft brown sugar
10 1/2 ozs vegetable oil
3 standard eggs — beaten
12 ozs brown self raising flour — sifted
2 teaspoon baking powder
2 teaspoons cinnamon
9 ozs grated carrot
3 ozs chopped walnuts
3 ozs mixed fruit

Mix together dry ingredients. Beat eggs in oil and mix into the dry ingredients. Pour into a greased lined tin 11 1/2" by 13 1/2" Bake at 320 F. 160 C. Gas Mark 2/3 for approx 1 hour.

Topping
1 200g tub light soft cheese.
2 tablespoons icing sugar
few drops vanilla

Mix well together and spread on top of cake. Dot with walnuts. This recipe makes 16 generous slices, perfect for a party or celebration. For a smaller cake, halve the ingredients.

Brandy Snap & Toffee

In October when a light mist descends and the nights start to 'draw in', the citizens of Hull lift their heads and sniff and say, "It's Hull Fair weather!" and in the middle of the month the trailers and vans, the Big Wheel, the Dodgem Cars, the old fashioned steam horses, the fortune tellers and all those who are there to entertain, descend upon Hull as they have done for hundreds of years. In Walton Street where the fair now stands, stalls are erected with balloons and streamers, glitter, toys and frivolous items which every child must have, and drifting on the air is the smell of onions, hot dogs and ketchup mingling with the sweet scented sugar spun candy floss and crisp golden brandy snap, which is taken home as a gift for those who are unable to take part in all the fun of the fair.

Brandy Snaps

2 ozs self raising flour
2 ozs sugar
2 ozs margarine
2 tablespoons golden syrup
1/2 teaspoon ground ginger
1 teaspoon brandy

Melt margarine, sugar and syrup in a pan; remove from heat, add other ingredients and mix well. Put teaspoons of mixture, set well apart onto a greased and floured baking tray and bake in a moderate oven 325 F 170 C Gas mark 3/4 for about 8/10 minutes.

Remove from oven and cool for one moment, then lift with a knife from the tray and whilst still pliable roll around the handle of a wooden spoon. If the mixture starts to stiffen too soon, place over heat to soften again. Put on to a wire tray to set. When cool, pipe or spoon whipped cream into each end.

Toffee

From Mr Thomas's 1907 Book of Recipes
(Sowerby Bridge)

1/2 lb brown sugar
1/4 lb butter
1 tablespoon water
1 teaspoon vinegar

Boil for twenty minutes in an enamelled saucepan, stirring all the time. Test it by dropping a spoonful into cold water; if the mixture is hard and crisp it is done. Pour into a well buttered tin. Thin slices of coconut or blanched and split sweet almonds can be added if liked, and should be laid on the buttered tin and the toffee poured over as they require no cooking.

Caramel Toffee

1 lb granulated sugar
1/2 lb golden syrup
3/4 lb butter
and a sixpenny tin of swiss milk

Stir for twenty minutes after it starts to boil, without stopping. When finished add one teaspoon vanilla, pour into greased tin and leave for about ten minutes, then cut into squares before it is quite cold.

Butterscotch

Mrs Ball Sproatley

1/2 lb butter
1 1/2 lb moist sugar
1/4 lb golden syrup
2 teaspoons water
1 teaspoon vinegar

Melt butter, then add sugar, syrup, water and lastly vinegar. Boil 20 minutes. Pour into greased tin and cut into squares before it is quite cold.

Savouries

In one of the old recipe books I was given, was a recipe for CHRISTMAS GOOSE. This was not any ordinary goose but a bird stuffed within a bird which was stuffed within another bird and so on and finally covered and cooked with a pastry crust on top. I then discovered that Mr Fox, butcher, of Malton, still continues with this old tradition. He starts with a duck which is then stuffed with a chicken, stuffed with a pheasant, then partridge and finally venison. Each bird is boned and a herbed stuffing set around each and finally tied or sewn, ready for roasting. A veritable task indeed, but a custom happily revived, for the CHRISTMAS POT is sent out to grace Christmas dinner tables all over the country.

I received a telephone call from Mrs Cranfield of Market Weighton who told me of the Giblet Pie which her mother used to make and which Mrs Cranfield also makes every Christmas. This was a traditional dish made in many farmhouse kitchens and was eaten cold on Christmas Eve. It was made up of as many giblets from as many hens, geese and ducks as possible for there were many hungry farmhands to be fed. We had a long chat of Christmas's Past, of Christmas trees brought in late on Christmas Eve, and of the children who gathered around to dress them with baubles and trimmings before they went to bed in excited anticipation of the following morning, when the house would be decorated with holly and mistletoe and the presents opened.

Giblet Pie

Neck, gizzard, heart and liver of any fowl.

Stew them until tender and remove the small bones from the neck. Season with salt and pepper and sprinkle with marjoram.

Make a good short pastry.

Put the meat and the liquid it has been cooked in into a deep dish and cover with pastry. Brush with egg and bake until the crust is golden. Leave in a cool place for the liquid to set to jelly and eat cold.

Potted Chicken Liver

Sometimes, chickens from the supermarkets arrive without their giblets and the liver is sold separately in plastic containers, but Free Range chickens from the butcher or the farm usually come intact.

8 ozs chicken liver.
1 tablespoon wine or dry sherry
1 clove of garlic
salt and pepper
tablespoon olive oil

Fry the chicken liver gently in the olive oil with the chopped garlic until the liver starts to change colour. Remove from heat. Add to it 1 tablespoon of wine or sherry and either put into bowl and mash with a fork or blend in a blender until smooth. Add salt and pepper to taste. Put into small ramekin dish, cover with foil and place in a dish or pan half filled with hot water and cook in a moderate oven for 15/20 minutes until set. Eat hot or cold with hot toast.

Chicken Liver Savoury

8 ozs chicken liver
2 tablespoons wine or dry sherry
4 ozs sausagemeat
1 egg beaten
1 clove garlic
salt and pepper
1 tablespoon cooking oil
handful of fresh herbs, marjoram/sage/parsley.

Fry the chicken liver gently in the oil with the chopped garlic until the liver starts to change colour. Remove from heat and put into bowl and mash with a fork. Fry the sausage meat, turning it over frequently until it starts to lose its pinkness. Remove from heat and drain off any excess fat. Put into bowl with the liver and garlic, add the herbs and wine or dry sherry, salt and pepper and beaten egg and mix well. Put into oven proof dish and cover with foil. Place the dish in a shallow pan or tray half filled with water and cook in a moderate oven for about 30 minutes until set.

Aislet

Mrs E Rainforth Hull
3/4 lb minced beef
1/2 lb sausage meat
1 slice raw ham
3 eggs (2 hard boiled and 1 raw)
salt & pepper
drop of milk
parsley

Cut ham into slices 1/2" thick. Put all meat into bowl, add salt, pepper and parsley. Beat egg with milk and add to mixture and stir. Grease a basin, half fill with mixture and lay hard boiled eggs on top. Fill with rest of meat mixture, cover with greaseproof paper and steam for 2 1/2 hours.

Beef Olives

Miss Gaukroger 1907

Cut slices of raw beef or steak, beat out quite thin with rolling pin and cover with a layer of breadcrumbs, mixed with a little parsley, onion, sage, pepper and salt. Roll up and place together in a covered stew pan with a little water; simmer gently for two hours then remove carefully, thicken the gravy and pour over the olives.

Pork Pie

Evelyn Cook, Holderness farmer's wife and author of GATHERINGS is a traditional cook and well known for her fine raised pork pies. This is her own recipe, perfected by her and in regular use for family and village events.

For the pastry
8 oz plain flour
8 oz self raising flour
1 teaspoon salt
6 oz lard
1/2 cup water

For the jelly
1 pint water
1 pigs trotter
pepper & salt

For the filling
1 1/2 lb roughly cut minced pork with good piece of fat minced with it.
pepper & salt & water

1 egg for glaze

Place minced pork in bowl. Season well and add about 4 tablespoons water. Mix well. Mix flour and salt in another bowl. Boil together lard and 1/2 cup of water in a pan, take off heat and add to flour. Mix with a wooden spoon and then knead with hands until pliable, keeping warm all the while. Roll out pastry and line greased medium sized loose bottomed cake tin. Fill with pork and roll out lid. Make hole in lid and seal edges firmly. Decorate with pastry leaves. Brush with beaten egg and bake in oven 350/375 F. 180 C. Gas Mark 4 for approximately 2 hours until golden brown and firm. Check with skewer to see if meat is cooked. Boil pig's trotter for about 1 hour with 1 pint water and seasoning, then boil rapidly to reduce until jellified. Allow both pie and jelly to cool slightly, then with a funnel add jelly through the hole in the pie lid. Leave until the next day when cold and set and remove from the tin.

Ancient Receipts

In the days before our dependancy on the National Health Service and modern medicine, people with ills and ailments often treated themselves with herbal medicines and special food rather than sending for the doctor. They made egg nog for nourishment, beef tea for strengthening, and used the fruits and hips of the garden and hedgerow for their natural vitamin C; they collected herbs and flowers, such as feverfew to cure headaches, valerian for nervous stress and wild thyme for sore thoats, coughs and colds and hangovers!

Robert Spofforth's Book 1724

Whilst researching in the County Archives in Beverley I came across a handwritten account book belonging to Robert Spofforth. At the back of the book was a selection of receipts and remedies, presumably written by Mrs Spofforth, Robert's wife or mother, I know not which. The book, still readable after over 270 years, transported me back through the centuries to a different age, a different life.

Cure for Ague

First purge by giving about Twenty Grains of Jallop in the morning of the day the fit is expected. Mix three ozs of Bark in a bottle of strong port wine and drink of it three or four times a Day. This receipt is from Mrs Kilvington.

Beef tea for convalescents

1lb gravy beef, 1 pint cold water, 1/2 teaspoon salt. Remove the fat and shred the meat finely. Place in an earthenware jar, add the water and salt and cover closely. Place the jar in a saucepan of boiling water or in a slow oven and cook for about 3 hours, stirring occasionally. Strain, remove carefully all traces of grease, and serve.

Blackurrant Geneva.

Take a quart bottle, fill it with very fine ripe Black Currants, cut them off the stalks singly, then pour in as much Geneva as the bottle will hold, cork it up close and after it has stood three or four months in a Moderate dry place, pour off the Liquor, bruise the berries in a Marble Mortar and squeeze them through a piece of cloth. A Tablespoon or half a Wine Glass is sufficient to take at a time, this must be repeated as occasion requires. Mix from Elizabeth Broadley.

Nettle Porridge
(Spring Medicine) 1850

Gather young spring nettles when about two inches above the ground. Wash and put into a pan of boiling salted water, a pint of water to a pint of nettles. Boil until tender. Then take out the nettles, chop fine and put back into the pan and thicken with fine oatmeal. Boil up and add a lump of butter and pepper. Eat with bread and butter or oatcakes for supper.

Pick Me Up Mixture

A little over a gill of rum, 2 tablespoons olive oil, 1/4 lb honey, 5 fresh eggs. Whisk eggs well together and slowly add olive oil, then honey gradually and lastly rum, slowly stirring all the time. Mix well and bottle. Half a wine glassful two or three times a day between meals or as it suits you.

During a visit to the Local History Library in Hull, I found a handwritten note book with the simple title, **Useful Receipts, 1889**. *Unfortunately the author hadn't left behind her name for posterity, but there were many remedies given for such diverse ailments as Gout, Dropsy, Corns, Baldness and others, including the following:*

Nutmeg is a most excellent spice to assist digestion.

Nutmeg also answers for headache — to be used in a little hot water; and — a thimbleful of whisky rubbed in the hand and held to the nose cures headache at once.

Bronchitis. Relieved by drinking very hot water.

1 lb Oatmeal gives a man as much strength as 3 lbs of beef.

Christmas Puddings

November was always an important month in country districts, for this was the time of Martinmas or Leaving Day and the Hiring Fairs. Farmworkers and servants who hadn't been kept on at the farms, packed their boxes and took themselves off to the Hiring Fairs in the nearest town or market, where they would hope to be lucky enough to be hired for the next twelve months. On this day, many farm wives cooked a dish of sausage, bacon or ham, with warm breadcakes to 'dip' in the fat or gravy; this tradition is still continued today in many Holderness farmhouses. On the last Sunday before Advent, servants went home to their families and found preparations for Christmas about to start. This day was known as 'Stir Up Sunday' when everyone took part in stirring the Christmas Pudding.

Whilst searching through old Yorkshire recipes I came across many for Plum Pudding. Some were over 100 years old and were richly filled with fruit, eggs, brandy and beer. Others which came later were more economical and used beer only and fewer eggs, six or eight instead of fifteen, and some were very frugal indeed and used no eggs at all, whilst others substituted potatoes and carrots for breadcrumbs and candied peel. The amount of ingredients seem huge by today's standards, but we have to remember that families in those days were much larger than today. The recipes given can be halved or quartered in quantity for a smaller pudding.

Plum Pudding

1 lb stoned raisins
1 lb currants
1 lb grated suet
1 lb stale breadcrumbs
1/2 stone flour (7 lbs)
8 eggs
1/2 pint milk
1/4 lb grated candied orange and lemon peel
1 oz powdered cinnamon
a little grated nutmeg
1/2 oz powdered ginger
a glass of brandy or rum
pinch salt

Mix the breadcrumbs, flour and suet in a basin. Beat the eggs and milk together and add, beating well with a wooden spoon. Stir in the currants and raisins and mix well. Mix in the the orange and lemon peel, cinnamon, nutmeg and salt. Next add the rum or brandy and mix well. The pudding is now ready to be baked or boiled, according to taste. If to be baked, butter your tin or basin, put the pudding in it and bake in an oven for nearly two hours. If to be boiled pour into a cloth. Tie the cloth, allowing room for it to swell and boil for six hours. Serve with rum, brandy or white sauce.

64

No Egg Plum Pudding

1 lb flour
1/2 lb grated suet
1/2 lb currants
1/2 lb raisins
1/2 lb sugar

Mix together the dry ingredients with a small bottle of stout, and add a little milk to give lightness. Place in greased pudding basin and steam for six to nine hours. Serve with sauce.

Christmas Pudding

Mrs Cranfield, Market Weighton
This 70 year old recipe is still in use today.

1 lb stoned raisins
1 lb currants
1 lb suet
1 lb treacle
1 lb plain flour
1 lb carrots
1 lb potato
1/2 lb mixed peel
pinch nutmeg

Grate potato and carrots and add to rest of ingredients. Stand until next day. Steam for 6 hours.

Rum Sauce

Mrs F Hirst, Huddersfield, 1924

1 gill cold water (1/4 pint)
2 oz castor sugar
rind of 1 lemon
1 teaspoon butter
3 tablespoons Jamaica rum
4 small drops vanilla
1 inch cinnamon stick
arrowroot

Place the water, sugar, rum, lemon rind, butter, vanilla and cinnamon stick in a small saucepan, mix well, bring to simmering point, then thicken with a saltspoon of arrowroot dissolved in a little water kept back for the purpose. Simmer for 1 1/2 minutes and strain into a hot sauce tureen. Serve with Plum Pudding or any steamed pudding.

Supper Dishes

Turkey, Courgette and Aubergine Mix

"Ah," I hear you say, "but aubergine is an exotic vegetable, not from Yorkshire!" True, it is, or at least it was, and just like the marrow, pumpkin and tomato which were brought in to England from warmer climes in the last century, so the aubergine has found a home here too. And although supermarket aubergines are often supplied from Israel and Holland, in glasshouses not a mile from my home, the aubergine is grown commercially for the home market. I too, in a good summer have successfully grown them in my unheated greenhouse along with the tomatoes.

For those who enjoy food, cooking is about experimentation, with the basic knowledge which we have learned from our forebears, and it is very satisfying to try something new to add to our collection of good things to eat. This recipe is so adaptable that it is possible to use whatever vegetables you have to hand, — carrots, leeks, etc, and you don't have to use turkey, — chicken pieces or tender beef can be used equally as well, or meat can be left out entirely. What it is really, of course, is an old fashioned hot pot, but cooked quickly in a pan on top of the cooker.

12 oz diced raw turkey
1 aubergine
2 courgettes/baby marrow
1 onion
1/2 lb fresh skinned tomatoes
2 cloves garlic
1/2 pint stock or 1 tin tomatoes in juice
1/2 cup wine or cider
salt and pepper
2 tablespoon sunflower oil

Slice the aubergine and courgette, put them in a colander, sprinkle with salt and leave for at least 10 minutes. Dice the onion and crush or chop the garlic cloves and fry gently in 1 tablespoon of oil until turning transparent. Add the diced turkey and quickly sear all over. Turn up the heat, add the other tablespoon of oil, squeeze out the excess moisture from the aubergine and courgette and add to the pan with the fresh tomatoes, stirring constantly until everything starts to sizzle. Add the stock or tinned tomatoes and the wine and bring to simmering point. Turn down the heat until the casserole merely trembles and cook for about 30 minutes. Before serving sprinkle with chopped fresh parsley. This is especially good with jacket potatoes.

Vegetarianism isn't new, there have been non meat eaters around for a long time.

Nut Potted Paste (1934)

1 oz haricot beans
2 oz shelled walnuts
pinch of salt and cayenne pepper
small lump of butter — walnut size

Soak the beans overnight, wash, boil well, drain and put through a mincer with the walnuts. Add seasonings and melted butter to make a paste. Mix well and put into jars with melted butter on top.

I tried this using a tin of ready cooked beans and whizzed it in my blender. It was ready in a matter of minutes and is a good vegetarian spread, with hot toast or biscuit.

Roasted Onions (1934)

Take six good size English onions and peel them. Put about 2 oz dripping or margarine in a pie dish and melt in the oven. Put in the onions and roast for about one and a half hours in not too hot an oven, and keep turning until they brown. When done they will be nice and juicy. Take off the outer layer of skin, add salt and pepper and a good helping of butter. These make an excellent dish for tea or supper, especially on cold nights and are good for a cold.

Courgette in Cheese Sauce

1 1/2 lb vegetable marrow/courgette/ onions/leeks
1 bay leaf
4 oz butter/margarine
2 tablespoons flour
1 pint milk
3 oz grated Wensleydale or Swaledale cheese
2 oz fresh breadcrumbs
salt and pepper

Roughly chop the vegetables and fry in 2 oz butter until tender, drain and place in warmed ovenproof dish. Make cheese sauce by adding flour to remaining melted butter and cook carefully for one minute. Remove from heat and slowly add the milk, stirring continuously until smooth. Simmer gently until sauce thickens. Draw off heat, add grated cheese and seasonings. Pour sauce over vegetables, top with fresh breadcrumbs and a little extra grated cheese. Place in medium oven until golden and bubbly and serve with creamed potatoes.

Cheese Pudding

1 medium onion
4 oz fresh breadcrumbs
4 oz crumbled Wensleydale cheese
2 eggs
3/4 pint milk
salt and pepper
chopped parsley
1/2 level teaspoon dry mustard

Chop the onion into small pieces, beat eggs with milk and cheese, add breadcrumbs, mustard, salt and pepper and stir well. If you have a blender whiz for a few minutes until smooth, otherwise leave to stand for 15 minutes. Transfer into a well greased baking dish and bake in a fairly hot oven 400 F. 200 C. or Gas Mark 6 for about half an hour or until firm and golden. Sprinkle with chopped parsley just before serving.

Root and Tomato Layer

1 lb swede
1 large potato
1 large carrot
2 oz butter
salt and pepper
For the sauce
1 medium chopped onion
12 oz tomatoes - tinned or fresh
1 oz butter
1/2 pint vegetable stock
1 crushed clove of garlic
1 tablespoon tomato puree
1 tablespoon fresh basil
salt and pepper

Chop vegetables and cook in boiling water until just tender. Meanwhile, make a tomato sauce as follows. Fry the chopped onion in melted butter until transparent. Add remaining ingredients and bring to the boil, reduce heat and simmer for 20 minutes until the sauce reduces and thickens.

Roughly mash the vegetables with butter, add salt and pepper, put into warmed serving dish, cover with the tomato sauce and serve at once.

You will notice that I have suggested Wensleydale and Swaledale cheese for some of the recipes given. This is because I am so pleased to find that small dairies are again surviving and there are dairies in North Yorkshire and the Yorkshire Dales who are once more producing excellent cheese made from cow's and sheep milk..

Fruits of the Earth
Apple Mint Sauce

This sauce can be made in larger quantities, when cool put into small containers and freeze.

4 large cooking apples. Windfalls will do fine.
2 sprigs of freshly chopped mint — about 8 leaves.
1 tablespoon sugar
squeeze of lemon juice
1 tablespoon water

Peel, core and slice the apples and put in saucepan with water and lemon juice. Cook over low heat to a soft puree. Remove from heat and add chopped mint and sugar, return to heat and stir until the sugar has melted and the mint is cooked through with the apple. Serve hot or cold with pork or lamb, and new potatoes.

Walnut Pickle

Walnuts, brine, vinegar, spice.

*We had an old walnut tree in our garden which used to shed its green husk onto the ground below, which then opened to reveal the wrinkled shell of the nut. Sadly, the tree came down one wild and windy night and gone was my opportunity to do something with the green nut. Having found a Receipt, however, in **The Little Book of Preserves and Pickles,** which a very old friend gave me many years ago, and which had belonged to his mother, I realise that I would never have found the time or patience to use it. But here I reproduce it in memory of those unflagging and industrious cooks of long ago.*

Make the brine by allowing half a pound of salt to each quart of cold water. Take young green walnuts, prick them well with a knitting needle and cover them with the brine for a week. Take them out, dry them and lay on trays in the sun until they turn black. Two days should accomplish this. Allow two ounces of mixed spice and half an ounce of root ginger to every quart of vinegar. Boil it for ten minutes. Put the nuts in earthenware jars and pour the boiling spiced vinegar over them. When cold, cover with a bladder and tie down. Keep for a month before using.

Tomato Chutney

I.C.B. 1916
1 lb sharp apples
1 lb tomatoes
8 ozs brown sugar
1 oz shallots or small onions
1 oz garlic
4 oz salt
1/2 oz ground ginger
1 small teaspoon cayenne pepper
1 small teacup sultanas
1 quart vinegar *.

Boil apples and tomatoes in 1 pint vinegar until tender, then add other ingredients and the other pint vinegar. Boil for half an hour and stir occasionally.

* When I tried this recipe I used my pressure cooker for quickness, and found I needed only one pint vinegar as the liquid doesn't reduce as much as when using an ordinary saucepan. The result was still excellent, — very thick, hot and spicy.

Blackcurrant Jam
From "The Little Book of Preserves and Pickles"

Four pounds of blackcurrants
Three pounds loaf sugar

Remove the stalks from the fruit, put the currants in a pan and add the sugar. Stand the pan at the side of the stove till the sugar is dissolved and the fruit juicy, then bring to the boil and boil gently for about thirty-five minutes. Pour into jars, cover at once and keep in a cool place. Cost 1/2d.

Bramble Wine (Mr Sherry)

Today when we make home made wine we are careful to sterilise our jars, use special wine yeast, rack it and fine it and measure the specific gravity to make sure the finished product compares equally well with the wine we buy from the wine merchant. Here is a recipe for a country wine which follows none of those rules but which I understand has been in popular use for many years.

Place alternate layers of ripe blackberries and sugar in wide necked jars and allow to stand for three weeks. Then strain off the liquid and bottle, adding a couple of raisins to each bottle. Cork lightly at first and later more tightly. The wine will keep in good condition for a year, having a flavour rather like that of good port.

Apple Wine

24 lbs mixed windfalls
1 gallon water
3 lb sugar (to every gallon of liquid)
yeast

Chop the apples into small pieces, put into large bowl, add the previously activated yeast and water. Keep closely covered and in a warm place. Leave for a week, stirring two or three times a day. After a week, strain the juice from the pulp and press the juice from the apples. Draw off a pint of the liquid and add to half of the sugar, stirring well, and add to the bulk of the juice. Put into fermenting jar. A few days later draw off another pint and add to the rest of the sugar, stir and return to the jar. Cover with a clean cloth or fit air lock. Leave to ferment for about four weeks. Strain when cleared and fermentation has finished and bottle. Leave for about six months when it will be ready for drinking.

Spiced Fruit Punch

1 tablespoon marmalade.
1 dessertspoon syrup
1/4 to 1/2 teaspoon ground ginger
1 tablespoon water
2 tablespoon orange squash
1 tablespoon lemon squash
1/2 pint freshly made tea, not too strong

Put marmalade, syrup, ginger and water into a pan and make hot but do not boil. Add the lemon and orange squash and the tea and serve very hot.

Sloe Gin for Christmas

The fruits of the blackthorn are blue/black with a dusty bloom which look most inviting but are acid sour. The sloe was used as a purge in medieaval times, but today is known for its excellence in making a most delightful liqueur. It is said that its flavour improves the longer it is kept, but in our house we have never been able to resist it for more than just a few months!

Gather a quantity of sloes after the first frost. Rinse and drain, then prick them with a fork or skewer. Weigh the sloes and put into jar and add same weight of sugar. Cover with gin. Stir every day with a wooden spoon until sugar dissolves. Keep for at least a month before drinking.

Elderflower 'Champagne'

Finally, before Mrs Scryven closes her kitchen door, she invites you to take a glass of her Elderflower 'Champagne' and drink a toast to enthusiastic cooks everywhere and to those who enjoy the results of their endeavours.

1 1/2 lb caster sugar
1 gallon water
2 tablespoons white wine vinegar
thin rind and strained juice of 1 lemon
6 large elderflower heads, snipped from the stem

Put the caster sugar in a large bowl, then add water and stir until dissolved. Stir in the vinegar, lemon rind and juice and flower heads. Cover with a clean cloth and leave to stand for 2 days. Strain through scalded muslin and pour into clean screw top bottles. Screw the tops on the bottles and leave to stand in a cool place for three weeks. Chill before serving and ease the tops off the bottles carefully to ensure that it doesn't effervesce as you open it.